The Presence of the Thei

T T,

The Presence of the Therapist uses clinical studies based on the author's publications over the past 18 years to illustrate work with severely distressed children. The reader is encouraged to enter a dialogue with the author to explore the many dilemmas and difficulties of working with a person who has become highly defensive or fearful as a result of what has happened to them.

The intricacies of the 'present' relationship and the impact of the therapist's personality on the therapeutic encounter are explored as a strand of the total therapeutic relationship. This is considered alongside the transference relationship and wise work with the network of adults (parents as well as fellow professionals), which together bring about transition in the patient.

The Presence of the Therapist is a highly stimulating account of psychotherapeutic practice. It facilitates careful and broad thought about the therapeutic process and relationship that will improve clinical practice. The practical advice on how to survive in this demanding work will be of great benefit to all psychotherapists.

Monica Lanyado is a psychoanalytic child and adolescent psychotherapist. She is co-editor, with Ann Horne, of *The Handbook of Child and Adolescent Psychotherapy: Psychoanalytic Approaches.*

The Presence of the Therapist

Treating Childhood Trauma

Monica Lanyado

Brunner-Routledge
Taylor & Francis Group

HOVE AND NEW YORK

First published 2004
by Brunner-Routledge
27 Church Road, Hove, East Sussex BN3 2FA

Simultaneously published in the USA and Canada
by Brunner-Routledge
29 West 35th Street, New York NY 10001

Brunner-Routledge is an imprint of the Taylor & Francis Group

Typeset in Times by Mayhew Typesetting, Rhayader, Powys
Printed and bound in Great Britain by TJ International Ltd, Padstow,
Cornwall
Paperback cover design by Hybert Design

This publication has been produced with paper manufactured to strict
environmental standards and with pulp derived from sustainable
forests.

British Library Cataloguing in Publication Data
A catalogue record for this book is available from the British Library

Library of Congress Cataloging-in-Publication Data
Lanyado, Monica, 1949–
   The presence of the therapist : treating childhood trauma / Monica
Lanyado. — 1st ed.
       p. ; cm.
Includes bibliographical references.
   ISBN 1-58391-298-3 — ISBN 1-58391-297-5
1. Child analysis. 2. Psychic trauma in children.
   [DNLM: 1. Psychotherapeutic Processes—Child. 2. Stress Disorders,
Traumatic—therapy—Child. 3. Professional–Patient Relations. WM 170
L296p 2004] I. Title.

   RJ504.2.L367 2004
   618.92'8914—dc21

                                                2003013785

ISBN 1-58391-297-5 (hbk)
ISBN 1-58391-298-3 (pbk)

In loving memory of Margaret Sampson whose presence
continues to mean so much to so many

For everything there is a season and a time for every matter under heaven:
a time to be born, and a time to die;
a time to plant, and a time to pluck up what is planted:
a time to kill, and a time to heal;
a time to break down, and a time to build up;
a time to weep, and a time to laugh;
a time to mourn, and a time to dance;
a time to cast away stones, and a time to gather stones together;
a time to embrace, and a time to refrain from embracing;
a time to seek, and a time to lose;
a time to keep, and a time to cast away;
a time to tear, and a time to sew;
a time to keep silence, and a time to speak;
a time to love, and a time to hate;
a time for war, and a time for peace.

Ecclesiastes 3: 1–8

Contents

Acknowledgements and influences

It was pure luck that I heard about the profession of child and adolescent psychotherapy while I was still at university and was able to start training at the Tavistock Clinic as soon as I graduated. The rigour, attention to detail and carefully considered observational skills that I soaked up during my Kleinian training formed the bedrock of my way of working. After qualifying I was extremely fortunate to have many years of supervision with Frances Tustin who, in her typically generous and free thinking way, encouraged me to develop my ideas about work with traumatised children and to write about them. She was a wonderful example of open-mindedness and curiosity about the many different ways that there are to think about psychoanalytic work and indeed life in general, and this attitude has had a great influence on my work.

Conversations with colleagues as well as reading about Independent, Jungian and Anna Freudian theory and practice have greatly enriched my way of conceptualising what takes place in the consulting room. This has enabled me to value these different approaches as well as to feel comfortable with the diversity of thought that is required when trying to work with a wide variety of patients. Winnicott's writings have been particularly helpful and illuminating for me and I have returned to them time and again and found more richness and resonance with my experiences in the consulting room on each occasion.

These influences have confirmed my view that psychotherapy with children and adolescents today cannot operate from a 'one size fits all' perspective. As a consequence, some of the ideas in the chapters that follow, which I hope the reader will feel stimulated by and feel free to play with, may be unusual to some but not to others.

Writing papers and now this book has provided me with many wonderful opportunities to discuss psychoanalytic psychotherapy with a number of generous and thoughtful colleagues. They have read the original papers, read the new versions of the papers that have become chapters in this book, and given me helpful and frank feedback, which I have valued greatly. Some have contributed clinical material or observational material that has been incorporated in disguised forms into the text. I am very grateful for all their contributions. In addition, there are many clinicians that I cannot name as a further protection of the confidentiality of their patients, but I hope that they know how much I have appreciated all that I have learnt from them.

There are some colleagues who have encouraged and supported me for many years and patiently read seemingly endless drafts of the same papers. I am very grateful to Dilys Daws, Judith Edwards, Juliet Hopkins, Ann Horne and Ann Hurry for their generosity in doing this. I would also not have been able to work with the intensity that was required on this book without the help (in so many different ways) of my assistant, Sheila Taylor.

I am very grateful to Isabel Menzies Lyth for reading, listening to and discussing the ideas in this book over many months, helping me to sharpen my thinking and have the courage of my convictions. Very special thanks go to Tammy Fransman, who has unreservedly and unstintingly discussed and read the many versions of the original papers, as well as all the chapters in this book, and helped me to be rigorous as well as imaginative in what I have written. Particular thanks go to Margaret Sampson and Martin Miller for encouraging and enabling me to try and express what I really think and feel.

Many thanks also go to the editors and team at Brunner-Routledge, particularly Joanne Forshaw and Nicola Ravenscroft, for their high calibre help, advice and professionalism at all stages of producing this book.

Throughout the period of seeing the patients, writing the original papers and now working on the book itself, I have had the good fortune of having a loving family around me that has sustained me and kept me buoyant. For this above all, particularly in the light of all the suffering I have been aware of in my patients, I am enormously grateful.

A note on confidentiality

As a psychotherapist, writing about the very private experience of what happens in the consulting room is a rather strange endeavour. It feels like facing inwards and outwards at the same time, simultaneously being both highly introspective about the therapeutic process and highly public in trying to communicate this process to the reader. Confidentiality and privacy are so vital to the trust that the patient feels in the therapist that it is very difficult to write about therapeutic experience unless there is a great deal of thought about clinical ethics (McFarland Solomon and Twyman 2003).

There are a number of ways in which this difficult issue has been addressed in my past publications and in this book. Above all, I hope that should by any chance a patient, relative or friend of a patient recognise anyone in my writings, they will feel that I have described what took place between us in a humane and respectful manner. The only reason for writing about the therapeutic process is to add to the knowledge, understanding and necessary debates that must go on within psychoanalytic practice, if it is not to be accused of being secretive and not open to scrutiny.

Practically, I have thought carefully about the issue of confidentiality at the time of writing, on an individual basis for each of the children discussed in this book. As the papers span a period of 18 years, there has been dramatic change in general professional guidance about how to protect patients' confidentiality. The internet was only in highly restricted use when three of the papers were written in the mid to late 1980s. At that time, papers published in professional journals were likely to be in very limited circulation. There was of course still careful attention to disguise patients' identities, but there was certainly less likelihood that patients would come across these journals. The situation is entirely different now, and this presents our profession with major dilemmas, which are constantly under discussion (Gabbard 2000; Tuckett 2000).

The question of whether patients can give informed consent to their therapy being written about is particularly thorny and complicated when considering child patients, where it is the parents or carers who have to be consulted. Advantages and disadvantages of asking for patient consent are discussed carefully by Gabbard and Tuckett, and Ann Horne and myself in the introduction to *The Handbook of Child and Adolescent Psychotherapy: Psychoanalytic Approaches* (1999). Consent given while therapy is in process may play a distracting part in the therapeutic relationship, introducing extraneous factors which relate to the therapist's needs rather than the child's. Requesting consent when therapy has finished can be a difficult and potentially damaging experience for patients and those close to them.

This issue has been dealt with in different ways for each of the patients discussed in this book, often where possible in consultation with colleagues who knew the child and family. In each instance, after considerable discussion, we have come to a decision about how best to deal with the question of confidentiality. In addition, as little personal history as possible has been given for each patient and a number of 'red herrings' inserted to obscure any personal data, without losing the essence of the clinical material itself. Some inconsistencies in the text may be due to this attempt to obscure identifying information. The editors at Brunner-Routledge have looked for any obvious slips which might be identifying. I hope that the outcome of these efforts is sufficient to safeguard each patient in this extremely important aspect of psychoanalytic psychotherapy.

Part 1

The presence of the therapist

Chapter 1

The presence of the therapist and the process of therapeutic change

When the psychoanalytic psychotherapist enters the consulting room trying to be 'without memory or desire' (Bion 1967), what aspects of the therapist are actively left outside the door and what does the therapist enter the consulting room 'with'?

Some of the answers to these questions are comparatively straight-forward and relatively uncontroversial. For example, the therapist actively tries to put aside personal preoccupations and concerns about his or her private life as well as thoughts about other patients, even though at times of worry or stress at work or at home this can be extremely hard to do. The therapist strives not to introduce his or her agenda into a session other than in highly unusual circumstances or in relation to practical arrangements. The therapist makes efforts to hold back his or her opinions about difficult issues that the patient is trying to resolve, as the therapist's opinions do not belong in the psychotherapeutic session in which the patient has to try to find his or her own solution. However difficult it is to meet these standards, it is still comparatively easy for the therapist to identify when these hall-marks of good practice have not been met, and to attempt to consciously improve on them. We are all human, and inevitably at times painfully aware of how difficult it is to meet these exacting standards.

The answers to my opening questions become increasingly difficult and controversial the closer they get to the inner world of the therapist. For example, the therapist tries to be as open as possible to the patient's communications – that is, the therapist tries to leave as many personal defences as possible outside the room. The therapist knows that his or her ego, in the way that it is popularly understood, does not belong in the room. Neither does the therapist's judgemental superego. It is difficult to do this and it requires a level of self-discipline and self-awareness that it can at times be hard to find. These are complex and subtle ideals to uphold, as their roots lie in aspects of the therapist's personality that it is much more difficult for the therapist to observe and identify, or indeed to try to change.

But it is still easier to think about what does not go into the consulting room with the therapist than to think about what does. While there are the obvious conscious skills, insight and knowledge that result from the many years of rigorous training and supervision that the therapist has undergone, there is always the question of how much the training analysis has helped the therapist to be aware of his or her weaknesses, strengths, defences, vulnerabilities and blind spots. The need for the therapist to continue to scrutinise his or her inner world, to sift the impact of the patient from the background noise of the therapist's personal domain, remains throughout the therapist's working life.

These lines of thinking contribute to the concept of the therapist trying to put the patient in the foreground, while seeing him or herself as offering a service to the patient, in the more old-fashioned meaning of the word. However, as psychoanalytic psychotherapists do not take any standardised tests or treatment programmes into the sessions but 'only' take themselves, the process of therapeutic change is particularly reliant on how the individual therapist uses his or her training, clinical experience and ultimately his or her self.

This is not an easy theoretical place to be, and it would feel much more comfortable to be able to believe that it does not matter *who* gives the therapy, or *who* gives the interpretation. However, common sense as well as personal accounts from therapists who have had experience of more than one psychoanalyst, confirm that therapy feels very different with different analysts.

These are difficult and problematic issues to address and yet it is timely to attempt to take this area of discourse within psychoanalytic thought to a new stage. Much of the theoretical discussion about the personality of the therapist, the new relationship and the formation of new attachment relationships within therapy, has taken place in the psychoanalytic literature based on work with adults (see, for example, Baker 1993; Holmes 1998, 2001). I think that work with parents and infants, children and young people has much to offer to this debate, and that there is a body of knowledge, observation and clinical acumen that can make an important contribution to psychoanalytic insight in this area. Much of this clinical knowledge has arisen from work with the kind of traumatised, abused and deprived children that form the bulk of the clinical population seen by child and adolescent psychotherapists today.

Face to face encounters with child and adolescent patients mean that not only are the therapist's facial expressions available for the patient to perceive, but so is the therapist's body language. While we know that these perceptions are read in particular ways by patients according to their pre-existing internal worlds, there is also a reality to what they read about their therapist. Not all therapists will respond in the same way to a patient, and the face and body of the therapist conveys a great deal of important information to the patient, whether the therapist wants this information to be conveyed or not. Additionally, therapists working with children and young people may actively have to set boundaries on reasonable behaviour in the room. They may find themselves being touched by young patients in an entirely appropriate manner for the patient's tender years, and may need to practically help young children – for example, helping them to wash themselves after very messy play. The therapist as a person is a very real presence and body in the room.

I think that it is important to try to understand how the 'presence' of the therapist functions in the therapeutic process. This is rather like the attempts to understand the complexities of the use of counter-transference in understanding the patient's communications. Indeed, some would argue that it is no different to this debate. But I feel that the debate can be expanded considerably by thoughts about the presence of the therapist, which are the leitmotif of what is explored in this book. The clinical studies gathered together here paint pictures and provide illustrations of this process in action and how it intertwines with the transference relationship. Based on papers published over the last 18 years about work with children who were referred for a variety of reasons, but who all had traumatic experiences underlying their distress, the questions of therapeutic technique and how therapeutic change emerges have been an organising theme.

I have come to the concept of the 'presence' of the therapist as a way of thinking about what the psychoanalytic therapist takes into the room, from a convergence of two different trains of thought. The first of these is inter-personal and unique to a particular relationship at a particular moment in time (Tronick 2003), which is why I think of it as the present relationship; the second is deeply personal, relating to what might be thought of as the essence of the individuality of the therapist, which try as he or she may, cannot be kept out of any human relationship.

The 'present relationship' is now captured by the frame by frame analysis of video material from a wealth of developmental psychology research in parent-infant communication, as well as in parent-infant psy-chotherapy (Baradon et al. 2001; Woodhead 2002). This video evidence of the minutiae of interpersonal perceptions and interactions which become a part of implicit (that is, unconscious) memory, is happening in the con-sulting room, just as it happens in ordinary life. While many of the perceptions will be based on previous good and bad experiences, they are not all based on the past. There has to be a way for novel, different, current experience to be processed as well, otherwise nothing could ever change in the internal world. I now hesitate to use the word 'new' experi-ence, because it is so easy to get into a semantic debate about what is 'new', in the context of ongoing human growth and development. Perhaps 'new' is somewhere well along a continuum of development from 'old' or past experiences into the present.

Another way of thinking about this is in terms of pathways or roadmaps in a lifetime's journey. Before a patient is referred to therapy, he or she is usually rather entrenched in following a route which seems to be going round in circles, or clearly in a direction that is destructive to self and possibly others. The patient comes for therapy because it is felt that nothing will change without treatment. After successful therapy, the patient is no longer going round in the same circles and feels set on a different course in life. The difference, which might have started with a very small change of direction at first, can lead to a big change in location over time.

It is in the fact that the therapist, while perceiving and trying to process the transferred relationships from the past, responds *differently* to the way in which important people in the patient's past responded, that the potential for therapeutic change lies. This differentness, which relates to the way in which the therapist listens and uses psychoanalytic insight to understand the patient's many forms of communication, takes place in the current, that is present, relationship between patient and therapist. This is not the same as offering a corrective emotional experience to the patient, which gratifies the patient's longings. For example, an important part of what the therapist may be offering that is different may be a refusal to gratify Oedipal longings, or infantile omnipotence which might have consciously or unconsciously been confirmed in relationships of the past.

The second train of thought that contributes to the concept of the 'presence' of the therapist relates to the difficult question raised at the start of this chapter. That is, that while it is fairly clear what the therapist leaves outside the room, when going into a session what is it that he or she takes in? It is certainly not all of the therapist's personality, but it is a kind of abstraction of it, a meta-level which relates to what might be thought of as the essence of the person and which cannot be kept out of *any* human interaction that the therapist engages in. This is very hard to define. It is better described, and I hope indirectly experienced and sensed in the pages of this book, through the accounts of therapy that follow this more theoretical chapter.

It is important to remember that there are established safeguards that protect patients from the possible and thankfully rare dangers of therapists who might misuse the professional therapeutic relationship. Poor practice can take place within work in the transference relationship as well as within work in the present relationship. The profession of child and adolescent psychotherapy has very rigorous selection procedures for prospective trainees, and careful monitoring of the trainees' work through seminar presentations and individual supervision. The training takes place within small groups or in one-to-one contacts with senior members of the profession and lasts on average at least five years. This puts in place very high standards regarding who is allowed to qualify as a member of the profession. On qualification, the therapist joins a profession with a strict code of conduct and an ethics committee to uphold it. Membership of organisations that have their own similarly rigorous code of practice, and an ethics committee that investigates breaches of good practice, are safeguards for other professions, such as psychologists and medical practitioners.

To return to the book itself. While each chapter can be read independently as a clinical study of a particular aspect of the treatment of traumatised children, there are a number of concepts which link them together which I hope it is helpful to outline here.

An eclectic approach and thoughts about the process of change in therapy

Perhaps I should start this brief overview of the key concepts that are used in this book by stating that an eclectic approach to theoretical concepts has been very clinically helpful and liberating to me. I do not have a problem in taking different useful ideas out of this theoretical 'bag of tools', as seems appropriate to the differing clinical situations encountered during therapy. These are some of the ideas that I find useful and will outline below: thoughts about the naturally occurring processes of growth and decay; different types of processes of change; moments-of-meeting in therapy; the therapist's personal signature; therapeutic attunement; the total therapeutic relationship; and therapists' reverie. For clarity, I have left a further group of ideas, which centre on thoughts about transitions, play and creativity to Chapter 5.

It is important to remember that patients, who in the past might have been thought to be unsuited to psychoanalytic psychotherapy, are now being helped because of a flexibility of approach and a willingness to adapt and apply psychoanalytic thought to new areas. Here I am thinking of parent-infant psychotherapy, work with severely deprived, traumatised and multiply abused children including refugees, work with multiply disabled patients, and therapy with children with autism (Sinason 1988, 1991, 1999; Daws 1989, 1999; Tustin 1990, 1992; Alvarez 1992; Hopkins 1992; Melzack 1999). Work with children, young people and their families requires this pragmatic approach in which if it can be seen that a change of technique seems to work, it is likely to be cautiously used first and theorised about a good deal later. This time lag can be considerable, with clinicians often working in very different ways from those that they believe to be 'orthodox', without sufficiently sharing their findings with colleagues. If they did, they might find that their ways of working are less unorthodox than they fear, and more in keeping with contemporary clinical practice. There is a pressing need to place these findings in the public arena, and this is one of the moving forces behind this book.

The first idea that I want to discuss is that therapy must be alert to, and continue to try to utilise, the natural processes of recovery and change that surround us. Within the natural world, we have many obvious illustrations of this. For example, in London where the four seasons are very evident, we never fail to emerge into spring with its wonderful flowering of bulbs and blossoms despite the darkness of the cold and gloomy winter that precedes it. Similarly, on a daily basis the light of day inevitably follows the darkness of night. Some may say these are just trite and somewhat sentimental statements. I do not agree. I think it is all too easy to lose sight of just how remarkable these processes are. They illustrate how we live in a world that is full of naturally occurring rhythms and changes. Nothing naturally stands still.

The ideas of ebb and flow, and movement in life as well as the possibility of a natural harmony within it, are prominent in our culture. This can be seen in the tremendous growth in the acceptance of 'natural' remedies and the worldwide concerns that are now expressed about the dangers of interfering with the harmony of our ecological systems. The corresponding view of emotional ill health rests on the assumption that this arises from an impediment, which stands in the way of the natural unfolding of processes of emotional growth and development. This is the view expressed by Winnicott whose writings on playing, creativity and the therapeutic process have had a great influence on my work (Winnicott 1971).

There are of course also natural cycles of decay as well as very power-fully destructive natural forces such as storms, earthquakes, floods and fires. Similarly, there are powerful destructive forces within all of us which even with the best of experiences in life have to become an important part of self-knowledge if a balanced way of living is to be achieved. Life is full of duality – of strengths and weaknesses, positives and negatives, creation and destruction, love and hate, war and peace, light and darkness. Detecting, accepting and understanding the destructive forces which act in opposition to the creative forces, and learning how to rein these forces in, is as vital as nurturing creative potential. The ebb and flow of both of these forces – creative and destructive – needs to be followed during therapy so that creative potential is increased and destructive potential reduced.

On reflecting on the therapeutic process itself, I have found myself thinking about two types of process of change. There may well be others. There is the kind of change that is built up from many tiny, quiet changes, which are incremental and essentially developmental. Hurry and her colleagues have discussed this in detail (Hurry 1998). For example, to return to thoughts about natural processes, this is rather like the gradual emergence of a daffodil from the darkness of the bulb in the soil. On a day-to-day basis, only very small changes are seen, and then only if they are looked for. But on a week-to-week basis there are dramatic changes, climaxing in the flowering of the plant. This is the kind of change that emerges from the quiet type of therapeutic 'holding'. In many respects this could be thought about as a therapeutic 'background noise' that is present all the time during the course of a treatment. Examples can be found in the case studies, particularly 'Lesley' and 'Derek' in Chapter 2, and 'Sammy' and 'Pete' in Chapter 6.

The second kind of process of change has more of a 'before and after' feel to it. By contrast to the quietness of incremental change, it could be thought of as 'noisy' and very noticeable change, rather like the climax of the plant flowering referred to above. It is important to note how impossible it is to separate the one kind of change from the other. In a negative sense, traumatic experience itself has this quality of dramatic change with the sufferer often expressing the feeling that he or she will never be the same again. For traumatised patients, this sense of the potential for discontinuity and catastrophic change in life is part of what needs to be addressed in therapy, so that change does not automatically remain equated with disaster. However, change in a positive direction can also feel like a terrifying prospect. Patients can cling to what they intellectually know to be destructive ways of living and relating, but feel too frightened of being without these familiar patterns to let go of them. This was the situation with 'Hilary' in Chapter 7, which led to the title of the chapter based on the well-known Bible story of Lot's wife, who could not let go of the past.

Thoughts about the fear of change and one of the ways in which this is overcome in therapy, relate to the significance in the therapeutic process of what Stern and his colleagues in the Process of Change Group in Boston have helpfully called 'moments-of-meeting' (Stern *et al.* 1998). They came to the conclusion that at these times the therapist and patient 'are meeting as persons relatively unhidden by their usual therapeutic roles, for that moment' (p. 913). They argue that these moments were identified as being the point at which meaningful change took place in the treatments that they studied. The kind of change that they seem to be referring to is the 'noisy' change which has a 'before' and 'after'.

Thinking about the present relationship, I think that it can be argued that the presence of the therapist and his or her ability to truly 'meet' with the patient at critical points in the therapy can be pivotal at these times. Trust in the therapist's capacity as another human being to bring about positive change may be the determining factor in a patient's (often unconscious) decision to do something different, which breaks old patterns of relating and behaving. These are the particularly intense times in therapy when the therapist may well feel that his or her 'heart reached out for' the patient and what the patient was going through. A very special kind of 'heart to heart' contact can be experienced at these times – which could be thought of as a form of emotional 'intensive care'. Many of the clinical studies in this book illustrate how powerful this experience in the present relationship can be in helping trauma patients to start to recover.

The Process of Change Group also describe what they call the 'therapist's personal signature' which is particularly present at such times. Teasing out exactly what is meant by these terms can be elusive. Stern and his colleagues try to put into words experiences that many psychotherapists are intuitively aware of as being, at the time, highly emotionally charged and loaded with potential for change, and which subsequently seem to have been turning points for the better in therapy. The question of how these processes of change relate to and intertwine with the transference relationship is discussed in more detail in Chapter 7.

With the rapid growth of research in developmental psychology, the concept of attunement between parent and infant/child as well as between therapist and patient has become widely accepted (see, for example, Stern 1985). In more everyday language, this is rather like the experience of being 'on the same wavelength' as another person and also describes the development of the unique relationship which takes place in every treatment which is a going concern (Tronick 2003). Getting onto the same wavelength as the patient can be extremely difficult and can also vary in intensity from patient to patient, and at different points in any particular therapy. It is part of the overall experience of being understood, which is not only verbal but also non-verbal and intricately linked with the processes of projection and introjection.

Having perceived, received and tried to understand a patient's communications, there are many interventions that therapists make. Many of these are outside the transference and counter-transference relationship but are nevertheless integrated with it as a part of what can be conceived of as the 'total therapeutic relationship'. Within the total therapeutic process, several strands can be identified. Currently I conceptualise three main strands in the total therapeutic relationship, all of which have specific therapeutic potential. They are the transference relationship process which projects relationships from the past onto the screen of the present; the present relationship process as described above; and the external management and holding of the therapy, which is also a form of therapeutic process, and vital to the working through, external support and continuation of the therapy for children and young people. This third strand of the process is more evident and significant in work with children and young people than in work with adults, but can become highly significant in circumstances where an adult patient needs hospitalisation. There may well be other processes within this whole.

An analogy may be helpful to explain what I mean about the ways in which these strands of the total therapeutic relationship work together. They are rather like three musicians playing in a trio: they all need to work together as creatively as possible without one trying to outshine the other. To take the analogy further, each musician has a different musical purpose and score and yet the interpretation and performance of the music will vary greatly from one trio to another. It is also highly likely that the same trio will also have good and bad days in terms of how well they perform the same piece of music. This analogy allows the 'personal signature' of the trio to emerge in the manner in which the 'music' of the therapy is interpreted. It also conveys the importance of the integration of the different strands of the total therapeutic experience so that this becomes more than the sum of its parts.

The last concept that I want to introduce in this theoretical chapter is that of therapeutic reverie. By this I mean the musing in the therapist's mind about what is going on in the patient's mind and the total therapeutic process. What is actually in the therapist's mind may well be a powerfully interacting concoction of observations, projective identification with the patient, and containment of the patient's projections, as well as the therapist's personal and professional associations to these contexts. In part this is the process that Bion (1962a) describes, of the therapist turning un-metabolised beta elements into thinkable thoughts through the use of the therapist's reverie. It can be thought of as a kind of slow cooking or incubation of these many contents until a point at which they are ready to be served, or hatched. Even then, the question of how to feed back the understanding or insight that has been gained is crucial, and depends on the therapist's sensitivity to the patient's ability to hear what has been under-stood. Alvarez (2000) has discussed how significant the choice of words in the 'grammar of interpretation' can be in helping patients to make the most of the therapist's insight. Additionally, many insightful interpretations may remain in the therapist's head because the patient would be unable to hear them in words. Whether the patient is able to sense this understanding non-verbally is an open question and implicitly present in a number of the case studies that follow.

The therapist's experience of working with trauma patients

Having said all this, I now want to turn to some wider thoughts about the difficulties of working with trauma patients, because despite the awful nature of trauma this is essentially a hopeful book. The clinical studies and reflections in the pages that follow are, I hope, more than anything a testimony to the ordinary, extraordinary and ever-changing processes of living. Children do find ways to move away from the traumatic past towards potentially happier futures. The stories that unfold and the experiences that take place in the privacy of the psychotherapist's con-sulting room often confirm the saying that 'life is stranger than fiction'. Life is also more beautiful, as well as at times more ugly than fiction, and frequently more moving.

It may seem odd to make these pronouncements at the start of a book about the treatment of trauma in children and young people. However, as it is my intention to focus on the process of change, with the hope that I may stimulate reverie and thought in the reader about how people recover from terrible experiences and events in their lives, the affirmation of the good things in life feels very appropriate.

I am well aware of the possible accusations that may be levelled at me of being defensive, and in denial of the cruelties and horrors of the lives that many people have to lead. I hope that the case studies that follow will illustrate that this is not so. One of the underlying patterns that I am intensely aware of, particularly when working with traumatised patients, is the determination of self-destructive and destructive cycles to repeat themselves. Helping patients to recognise when they are entering this vicious cycle again, and then enabling them to find a different way out of the cycle, is a key part of the therapeutic process that leads towards some recovery.

What I am trying to reach towards in these pages is a description of a therapeutic stance that can remain in touch with the great pleasures that can be enjoyed in life, while understanding and facing, in a compassionate and forbearing way, the pain that patients bring to their therapy. This attitude, of necessity, includes an understanding of the intransigence and persistence of negative ways of relating, and of how enormously difficult it can be to let go of these entrenched patterns. I often find myself thinking about these internal adversaries as being evidence of the 'shadow' side of human nature, as described by Jung (1964), and find it important to be alert to the times when this aspect of the patient's personality is in the ascendance. Through this awareness I have developed a very healthy respect for the power of what is contained in this shadow part of human nature and how important it is to constantly hold this awareness in mind.

There is something deeply mysterious about what happens in this dark side of the human soul. At the same time as harbouring despair, misery, pain and hardship, it also holds a strange potential for change. It is after all only when people find themselves caught in this place for too long a time, with no sense of any light at the end of the tunnel, that they seek out psychotherapeutic help. And even then, as therapists we can offer no immediate or guaranteed relief – only the offer to try to help them to bear their suffering in less destructive ways, and to help them to find some acceptance and understanding of what is happening in their lives. Trusting in this process as leading to healing and growth is our greatest asset. Part of the therapist's skill lies in his or her understanding of the way in which these processes work, together with his or her ability to help patients to engage with this process.

Trying to establish and maintain an internal equilibrium on the pleasures and pains, hopes and despairs of life is difficult and challenging. One way of meeting this challenge is by attempting to make the effort as grounded as possible while retaining a broad and philosophical perspective on life. Naturally, this view can be applied to the therapist as well as to the patient, for it can be argued that if the therapist has not (and does not) continue to do their best to keep a balanced view on life, it becomes extremely difficult to help the patient to do the same. Of course there will be times when the therapist becomes despondent and despairing about the suffering that he or she encounters in the course of this work, but it is particularly at these times that the 'buoyancy' of the therapist is of greatest importance. It is natural to feel weighed down at such times by heavy emotions, but it is through the therapist's ability to 'bob back up' again that patients will feel sustained and accompanied through these dark periods of their lives.

Currently, with levels of stress within the workplace running high, the pressures from the work itself combined with the pressures to meet government targets can at times feel insurmountable. The children and young people themselves bring terrible histories of substantiated and repeated traumatic experiences, often at the hands of those whom they should have been able to look to for protection. The risk of the therapist becoming overwhelmed, burnt out, deeply depressed or highly defensive in response to trying to help these children and young people may be increasing. I have written in some detail about stress as an 'occupational hazard' for psychotherapists (Lanyado 1993), and take very seriously the need for therapists to ensure that they *do not* consistently overwork and that they *do* make sure that their leisure time really replenishes their emotional reserves.

There is a well known saying that it feels appropriate to paraphrase here. Fostering an ability to 'accept the things that cannot be changed, but have the courage to try to change those things that can, as well as have the wisdom to know the difference' plays an important part in therapists' efforts to maintain their emotional equilibrium. Superhuman efforts cannot be sustained. Ill health is one of the results. Traumatisation of the therapist who spends too high a proportion of their clinical time working with severely traumatised patients is an everyday risk. When the work takes place within a climate which does not support and contain the therapist in this extremely demanding task, the therapist's vulnerability to stress-related illness is increased. This is why the therapist needs to take real breaks from work at weekends and during holidays, and needs to nurture an active emotional life and leisure activities within these breaks. Opportunities to discuss the work with colleagues as well as regular supervision are also essential in the long term to the clinician's ability to continue with the work.

It is hard to sustain this work, and it is important to appreciate that therapists need to gather the strengths of a marathon runner, not a sprinter. This is a process which continues throughout the therapist's working life, in which a fuller awareness and understanding of how intricately the therapist's 'essence' is involved in the work can only be to the patient's and the therapist's benefit.

Chapter 2

Beyond words: the quiet presence of the therapist[1]

Feelings of terror, fear and helplessness in response to trauma are profoundly human responses to events that are experienced as life-threatening to the self and others. Alongside these emotions, there are bodily responses such as trembling, a pounding heart, an inability to speak or move and a difficulty in breathing, all of which dramatically indicate the indivisible link between feelings, body and mind. During more normal life experiences it is easy as a psychotherapist to forget about the body. The treatment of trauma will not allow this to happen.

My interest in the technical difficulties of treating traumatised children started with the two children with whom this chapter is concerned. At the time that the original paper was written in the mid-1980s, there was surprisingly little psychoanalytic literature about the treatment of trauma in children. The extent of physical, sexual and emotional abuse that we are now so well aware of was not known at that time. Clinically, I think it is probably fair to say that the emphasis was mainly on the child's internal world first and foremost, and that this led to a technical emphasis on the centrality of interpretation in bringing about psychic change.

Lesley and Derek were therefore very unusual patients at the time. Lesley, who was 9, was referred to me very soon after being raped. She had lived an entirely ordinary life until this point. Derek was referred to me many years after probably witnessing the murder of his mother by her partner, who was subsequently imprisoned. It happened that I was seeing both children at roughly the same time, which was what made the

---

1 Many of the ideas as well as the clinical examples in this chapter were originally published in 1985 as 'Surviving trauma – dilemmas in the psychotherapy of traumatised children', *British Journal of Psychotherapy*, 2(1): 50–62. The observation of the therapeutic value of a particular form of quietness in the therapist has been helpful to me since this time. My current thinking and understanding of why this is so have led to the expansion of the original paper into this chapter.

similarities in the therapeutic process so interesting to me. Despite their backgrounds and external traumatic experiences being so very different, rather than finding myself verbally helping them to reconstruct what had happened to them – that is, helping them to talk – I found myself and my patients becoming quieter and *less* verbal as the treatment progressed. The different qualities of the quietness, stillness and silence that we shared during their treatments stimulated the ideas presented in my 1985 paper on the technical dilemmas of helping traumatised children.

Thinking about these children now, I am still intrigued with why this quietness is so valuable, and have further ideas about why this might be so. I have been significantly helped in my thinking since writing the paper by the exciting convergence of developmental psychology, neuroscience and psychoanalysis, which raises new hypotheses about ordinary development as well as pathological development, and in particular trauma. My knowledge in developmental psychology and neuroscience is limited, but there are some findings which make sense of my earlier clinical observations that during the quiet periods of therapy something deeply healing can be taking place. This is not to say that there may not be other findings that would contradict those that I have found so confirming. However, it is in the convergence of different disciplines that exciting lateral thinking and new ideas can be generated. As well as psychotherapeutic practice gaining from the researches of developmental psychology and neuroscience, clinical experience and observation (particularly with infants, children and young people) have much to offer as hypotheses generators for further research. This is not a one-way exchange of knowledge.

In particular, the ideas that I have found most helpful in relation to the treatment of trauma are, from neuroscience, studies on affect regulation (Schore 1994, 2002) and, from developmentalists, theories about interpersonal interactions, attunement and moments-of-meeting (Stern 1985; Stern *et al.* 1998). These concepts are woven into the fabric of the clinical studies that follow. The concept of the brain as the organ of the mind that resides within the human body, which in turn exists within a complex pattern of human relations, suddenly seems a rather revolutionary and yet very obvious idea. The brain and the body are back at the centre of psychoanalytic thinking in a manner which goes back to Freudian roots. There is much that is not understood, but the convergence of ideas frees up thought about how the brain and body of one person can communicate unconsciously (or perhaps just outside consciousness, due to the tiny non-verbal cues which the body registers while the mind does not), with the brain and body of another person. Non-verbal communication is now located in the body, and clinical experience and observation – which has been so hard to validate in classical scientific terms – might now begin to gain more credibility outside clinical circles.

Having made these preliminary comments, I will now move to some thoughts about the impact of individual traumatic experience on relationships, before describing the clinical experiences with Lesley and Derek which so intrigued me all those years ago.

The impact of trauma on the individual and on their pre-existing relationships

Sometimes traumatic events happen to individuals; sometimes they happen to small or larger groups of people – family, friends and communities. The response of those who have not been traumatised to a survivor of trauma is complex. On the one hand, there is a tremendous urge to rescue and protect the survivor from further distress; on the other hand there is a horror in knowing too much about what the survivor has experienced. For example, people often don't know what to say to a young couple who have suffered a stillbirth, or how to talk to a suddenly bereaved friend. It is difficult at these times to find words to convey what is felt. The traumatised person may just want to talk and talk about what happened, and what they have to say is often unbearable for the listener to hear. The listener can often only bear to hear so much before they in turn begin to feel somewhat traumatised and even contaminated by association with the traumatised person. What can one say to such distressing outpourings and how close can anyone bear to be to this suffering and fear? Words of comfort on their own can feel so terribly inadequate.

There is also a completely different scenario in which the traumatised person may feel quite *unable* to talk about what happened and how he or she feels. At these times those who know them are for different reasons unsure of what to say. Should they mention the trauma, or should they not? Is it callous to talk about the trauma and then carry on with everyday mundane activities, or is this just what is needed? Are some things really better left unsaid, or is there a time and a place for everything? The well-known quote from Ecclesiastes 3:1, turned into a popular song in the 1960s and given in full at the front of this book, expresses this idea very clearly: 'For everything there is a season and a time for every matter under heaven: a time to be born, and a time to die; a time to plant, and a time to pluck up what is planted'.

One of the responses within the Jewish community to the traumatic experiences of the Nazi Holocaust was not to speak about it other than in highly restrained ways, until the next generation had grown. This was partly a deliberate and personal decision taken by many parents not to pass the trauma on to their children, to try and give them as normal a life as possible. But it was also a deeply unconscious decision relating to the unbearableness of what had happened, that could not be put into words. In the immediate aftermath of the Second World War, many children of this new generation grew up under the dark shadow of the Holocaust without knowing what it was. David Grossman (1994) captures this atmosphere vividly in his novel *The Book of Intimate Grammar*.

Eventually this new generation became able to know about and try to talk about what had happened. But it was often left to *their* children to be able to bear to think about what had happened in a more cogent manner, perhaps because the traumatic events were finally far enough removed from them in time and emotionally to be tolerable. Much has been written about the impact of trauma through the generations (for example, Bergman and Jucovy 1982). The immediate responses to surviving trauma – relief, survivor guilt, jubilation, despair – are just that: immediate responses. What happens over time – a lifetime as well as through the generations – is quite a different issue. And as with the example of the Holocaust and no doubt the impact of similarly terrible events on other communities, it can take generations for the shock waves of trauma to be dissipated in such a way that it becomes part of a community's history, contributing to the distinct character of each such community. Should the treatment of trauma, particularly in children, be accepting of the appropriateness of different therapeutic needs at different stages of recovery? Is there a time for silence as well as a time for talking?

The effect of traumatic experience on relationships between the survivor and those who were previously close to or knew them is inevitably profound. One of the starkest aspects of this impact is the way in which, if the trauma has happened directly to just one person, that person suddenly feels isolated from and very different to those around him or her. There is a 'before' and 'after' sense to even the closest of relationships, with the trauma as a catastrophe at the pivotal point of this change. It is as if the impact of the trauma has opened up a gulf between the survivor and his or her loved ones.

One of the less palatable, yet probably necessary ways in which we all respond to contact with people who have been traumatised is to defend ourselves from any impact on our inner selves. We tend to behave as if trauma is catching – as indeed, on an intra-psychic level, through the process of projective identification, it is. Being with someone who has been traumatised and is in a highly anxious and agitated state will also physically arouse the listener so that the listener's sympathetic nervous system is activated. This can be experienced, for example, as higher heart rate, increased bodily tension, a wish to act (fight), or a wish to cut off or end the contact with the traumatised person (flight). There is also likely to be an increased level of anxiety in the listener because of the evidence from the trauma survivor that life can be so dangerous to anyone – which of course includes the listener. No wonder it is so hard to listen. Simply reading about the experience of some of the children in this book is likely to have a similar effect.

Thinking purely practically, there is also the reality level of the experience. If one member of the family is severely traumatised and cannot function, there is a great need for the rest of the family to remain emotionally healthy to help the survivor to recover. They have to try to get on with life and perhaps temporarily take over some of the functions that the trauma survivor cannot fulfil in the immediate aftermath of the trauma. The net effect of all these responses can be that at a time when the survivor so badly needs to feel the authentic presence of others, such a large gulf may open up between him or her and those who care, that the sense of isolation of the sufferer becomes unbearable in itself. This terrible sense of loneliness and hopelessness can significantly contribute to the risk of suicide.

Trauma survivors can readily accuse those close to them, including their therapists, of not being able to understand them because they have not experienced the same trauma. 'You don't know what it's like' is often a true statement and in my view is best met with some recognition of this truth. However, there is also the caveat that not knowing 'what it's like' does not mean that the therapist or any other person is not willing to listen, or that there is not also a strength in this listening by a non-traumatised person which is potentially deeply healing.

The problem of what I have come to think of as trauma patients becoming emotionally 'untouchable' was highlighted for me by the two patients discussed in this chapter. The 'untouchables' are members of a hereditary Hindu caste who are felt to defile and contaminate members of higher castes on contact. A sense of recoiling in horror at what the trauma survivor has experienced is very common, and very human. Psychotherapists are not immune to this defence and the difficulty of developing an intimate relationship with the traumatised patient is likely to be a central part of the therapeutic process of change (Garland 1998). It is this problem that is primarily addressed in this chapter. For the purpose of clarity, many other important and interesting concerns relating to the treatment of trauma have been put to one side, although they are in reality interrelated (see, for example, Hopkins 1986; Pynoos 1992; Emanuel 1996; Grunbaum 1997; Mendelsohn 1997).

When a child has been traumatised, there will be disruption of ordinary emotional developmental processes at the very least and there could well be some arrestment of these processes or regression to earlier developmental stages. The child has truly been knocked off balance – if that balance was there before the traumatic event took place. If that balance was not there (as with most of the children discussed in this book), it is even harder for the child to find his or her way towards a healthy developmental pathway. The younger the child, the more likely that brain function will be affected in such a way that chronic states of fear become character 'traits' (Perry *et al.* 1995). Additionally, because of the child's continued appropriate dependence on the parents in particular, and their caregiving and protective role and instincts, the impact of the child's traumatic experience on family dynamics is enormous. Many parents irrationally (and omnipotently) blame themselves for not having been able to protect their child from serious illness, accidents or violent or sexual attacks. On an equally irrational level, many children blame their parents for the cruelties and dangers of the world that they had previously been unaware of, and after the trauma feel they were not adequately protected from.

Despite all of these difficulties, it is important to remember that the vast majority of trauma survivors are nevertheless helped to live with what has happened to them, by the love and support of those who deeply care for them. Only very small numbers find their way to a psychoanalytic psychotherapist. When they do, what is it that can be offered to them, to help them to start to recover from the impact of the trauma?

One way of thinking about this process is to recognise the problem of their emotional untouchability and how this impairs the trauma survivor's ability to use the love and support that exists for them in their everyday lives. By becoming receptive to the communications that those closest to them cannot bear to receive or are unable to receive, the therapist can try to bridge the emotional isolation and help to detoxify some of the worst thoughts, feelings and memories by having them known by another person. This involves a way of listening which some people, including therapists, are able to offer – being very present and listening with the heart, body and soul, which can help the trauma survivor to feel less alone in their suffering. What is listened to is often non-verbal, when unconscious to unconscious communication is taking place through projective identification. This is not as fanciful as I might have once thought (although nevertheless intuitively believed). Frame by frame analysis of video material of ordinary parent-child interaction, as well as of parent-infant psychotherapy, illustrates the minute physical cues that are no longer registered in conscious perception and yet are encoded in implicit (unconscious) memory. These are body memories, which link to the physical and emotional 'presence' of the listener – be this a therapist or any other intimate 'other'.

As well as listening in this very present way, it is important to find a way to reach out to the trauma survivor without frightening him or her further, while maintaining a healthy respect for the defences that are being used to keep the person safe – particularly if they seem extreme. From feeling so terribly alone, the trauma survivor may then gradually start to feel able to relate to others again. This process of finding a way to get alongside the trauma sufferer owes much to the Winnicottian concept of 'being alone in the presence of someone', as well as the creative and healing processes that Balint postulates as taking place in the area of the basic fault (Winnicott 1958; Balint 1968). Bowlby has a similar emphasis when writing about the application of attachment theory to the psychotherapeutic process, in which he sees the therapist as a 'companion to the patient in his exploration of himself and his experiences' (Bowlby 1988: 151).

Lesley and Derek brought the problem of emotional untouchability home to me. I found that as their therapy progressed I spent considerable amounts of time in a state of mind that I could only describe as 'therapeutic reverie'. This happened not only during the therapy sessions, but also between sessions, particularly when they were in deeply regressed states. This therapeutic reverie was not a sentimental state, although it certainly contained a great deal of the compassion that is often felt towards patients who are in terrible distress. It also contained many awful thoughts, feelings and fantasies about what they had experienced, particularly during the early stages of their therapies, when my most important function seemed to be finding a way to listen to them and get closer to them. During this early phase, I came to realise that it was also helpful that I gradually facilitated the conditions that could provide the quietness and peace of mind that they seemed to need and which felt healing to them. At times this experience was very much like sitting quietly at the bedside of somebody who is very ill and trying to nurse him or her calmly and confidently back to health. I needed to find a way of being close to them but separate from them, while remaining able to survive knowing about the depths of the feelings which resulted from their traumatic experiences.

Much of this process took place within what I would now think of as the present relationship. By using the word 'present', I have in mind that I attempted to be very 'present' for these patients, particularly during their prolonged silences, as well as the contemporary (present) part of our relationship, as distinct from the transference relationship strand. Being 'present' in this way was the result of the current interaction in the room, my attempts to be sensitively attuned to both patients in a manner that was unique to each particular relationship, and the quality and content of the reverie that I found myself in (Ogden 1999).

Lesley

The initial meeting with Lesley's parents suggested that she had been a sociable, well-balanced, healthy child before she was raped. She had been a secure 9-year-old little girl who had been horribly changed by the rape and was terrified to be on her own at all. She suffered nightmares and flash-backs and had great difficulty attending school. She didn't want to see her friends and only wanted to be with her mother. She had to sleep in her mother's bed and her father had been ejected to the spare room. I saw Lesley twice weekly and her parents met with a colleague once a week throughout her therapy.

In the early days of therapy, Lesley was numbed by what had happened to her and confused by the effect it clearly had on everyone around her. She felt that she had become a weird kind of celebrity overnight, and could not cope with the odd kind of specialness that was accorded her by well-meaning friends and people in the community. Although her name never appeared in the media coverage of the rape, she felt that everyone knew that it was she who had been raped. She felt deep shame about this. Her mother, whom Lesley described as having been 'joyful' in the past, was broken and irrationally blamed herself for what had happened. Her father, by temperament a dependable and gentle man, had expressed violent feelings towards the man that the police had arrested, and who was subsequently convicted. As my colleague put it, in effect the whole family had been raped.

Lesley felt it was her fault that her parents had become transformed in this way. She suddenly feared that she could unwittingly have a powerfully destructive effect on anyone who had been close to her – or tried to become close to her. It gradually emerged that she was frightened that I would also be damaged if I became close enough to her to know about what she was going through, and so she very deliberately kept me at a distance. At the start of therapy, Lesley was able to talk in dribs and drabs about what had happened to her, but unable to talk about any of her feelings relating to the rape. As time went on, she became even *more* unable to talk about the trauma, rather than less. However, I was always intensely aware that underneath this defensiveness she was emotionally raw and terribly vulnerable.

While Lesley could not talk to me, she communicated powerfully on a non-verbal level, and my head became filled with imaginings about what had happened to her. At the same time, it is probably accurate to say that my heart became full of the undigested feelings of terror, panic and horror that she was living with. The fact that she didn't use words to communicate did not clinically feel like a significant issue to me. My clinical intuition suggested that this was not yet the time for words. I was also not convinced that in the face of her resistance to using words, talking was necessarily the key to helping her recover at this stage in her young life. Part of my task was to try to help her find the words for what she was unable to put into words when she first came to see me. However, these might be words that she never uttered to me or anyone else, but that she used within herself when she needed to; words which helped to bind and process some of the unspeakable terror that she had experienced.

Containment of the trauma, therapeutic reverie and the emergence of the transitional space

While Lesley was unable to talk about the rape, I increasingly found that I spent the sessions, as well as some time between sessions trying to piece together in my mind what had happened to her. Lesley, the rape and what she was going through in the present, would come into my mind at all sorts of unlikely times in what I came to think of at the time as a therapeutic reverie. Looking back on this, I now think of this as my having had Lesley 'in my pocket', in the same way that many years later another patient who had reached a point where she found life unbearable was also, for a while, 'in my pocket' ('Hilary' in Chapter 7).

I do not think that this is unprofessional or illustrative of a lack of boundaries. I think it is indicative of a particular aspect of the therapeutic process that as psychotherapists we inevitably carry from time to time, particularly when the patient is filled with hopelessness and a wish to die. It cannot and probably should not be switched off between sessions. At its height, in my experience, it does not last for more than a few weeks at a time. I agree with Carpy (1989) that, at certain times, recognising this process as being a necessary part of the present therapeutic relationship that needs to be actively alive within the therapist, as a counterbalance to the deadness within the patient, helps this difficult experience to become more acceptable and tolerable for the therapist. This important aspect of the counter-transference experience is discussed in more detail in subsequent chapters. The dangers are that the therapist can get stuck with experiencing this counter-transference experience and be unable to reflect on it. The role of colleagues and supervisors in helping therapists to regain a thoughtful perspective on what is happening at these times can be vital in the processing and transmuting of the counter-transference experience into a therapeutic experience for the patient.

I gradually came to understand that this therapeutic reverie, based mostly on non-verbal communication, was highly significant in facilitating Lesley's recovery. I put very little of this disturbing reverie of mine into words, but Lesley seemed to experience my quiet, contemplative state of mind as an opportunity to have her unspeakable distress received and heard at a very deep level. The silences we shared gradually became filled with anguish and despair. Often simultaneously, she expressed intense hostility towards me for not allowing her to retreat into herself or abandon all attempts at continuing her life.

At times she hated me for, as she now experienced it, putting her through the pain of her therapy. In her perception, *I* was now the cause of her pain, not the man who had raped her. This was the transference strand of the therapeutic relationship, which bought her a step closer to hating and expressing her rage with the rapist. It was a sign of her reviving psychic buoyancy. In terms of the present relationship intertwining with the transference relationship, the fact that I, as her therapist, could survive and remain constant in my attempts to be with her, despite her hostility towards me, helped her to feel safer with me and more in touch with her deepest feelings. This was a hostility that she could not express fully towards her parents because of their broken state and her irrational guilt that it was she who had damaged them.

This was the therapeutic scenario into which Lesley introduced a game, which in various forms she returned to throughout the rest of her therapy. It was indicative of a freeing up within her of her creative abilities – what I would now recognise as the beginnings of her ability to move into a 'transitional play space' (which is discussed in greater detail in Chapter 5). The creation of this transitional space had come about gradually, possibly as a result of an accumulation of experiences of 'being alone in the presence of the therapist' which had taken place during many of the quiet and silent times we had shared in the sessions (Winnicott 1958). It had emerged from the interaction, in the present relationship between us, and was uniquely created between us, in a way that made it neither hers nor mine – the classic qualities of a transitional phenomenon as described by Winnicott (1951). During these quiet and more peaceful times, Lesley was both able to be alone and yet not really be alone at all, as I was very present. A shift was gradually taking place between the times when she felt so isolated that she wanted to die, more ordinary loneliness and separateness, and the in-between place where she could bear, in small doses, to be alone with herself.

In her first piece of freer play in the therapy, Lesley took some small wooden houses and lined them up, calling them a train. The train chugged around until it became a town, then became a train again and finally a town which this time was next to the sea. Lesley used marbles to represent the motion of the sea. The marbles rolled all over the place and threatened to (in her words) 'flood the town and wreck it'. To stop this happening, she used small plastic fences to make a kind of sea wall to keep the marbles in place. I knew from the early therapy sessions that one of the reasons Lesley would not talk about the rape was that she was terrified she would lose all control, start screaming hysterically and not be able to stop. She had been gagged at the time of the rape. With this in mind I very cautiously, a step at a time and watching her response carefully, interpreted to Lesley that possibly the potential flood of madness that she felt she could barely hold back was beginning to be experienced as held by me, the 'sea wall' in her therapy. She was able to accept this piece of understanding without being overwhelmed by it.

It is striking to note how this clinical material reflects recent neuro-scientific research on affect regulation and how the brain becomes flooded by stimuli (and literally by neuro-chemicals) when there is traumatic experience or any trigger which prompts memories of the trauma (Schore 1994, 2002). The skill of the therapist from this point of view lies in their ability to 'affect regulate' – that is, to gradually lower the level of arousal through the interpersonal therapeutic relationship. My intuitive emphasis on quietness and stillness, rather than trying to approach anxieties that were heavily defended against, would therefore be in keeping with this research. Perry et al.'s (1995) findings, in which the suggested therapeutic aim is to minimise the stimulation of the neural pathways that communicate the fearful affects of trauma in the hope that these pathways may eventually fade through lack of use, also support this view.

Lesley's game developed many variations but she never asked me to join in. It seemed that she needed me to watch this game and indeed to facilitate its happening. In its most repeated form, the marbles were put inside the perimeter of the wooden houses, so that they were held in place, and then carefully and skilfully the houses were removed and every attempt was made not to let the marbles move. Over the months, this game was understood as representing her continued attempts to contain her own unthinkable, awful feelings and memories, facilitated by my containing them through her projections and my subsequent reverie about them. There were many times when I felt quite shut out and redundant when Lesley played these games, as they could at times become highly obsessional and defensive, in the way that her drawings had been in the past. However, as there was a level of absorption and concentration about the games which impressed me, I realised that even though they sometimes felt (and were) defensive to me, they were clearly very important to Lesley. In the main, the quality of Lesley's absorption in the games reminded me of ordinary, healthy play in children, where the experienced parent knows not to interrupt because the child is truly busy with important internal matters. This is the kind of play which, when it emerges in therapy, is precious and needs to be given as much space to grow as possible, with as little interruption as possible from the therapist. It is an achievement.

I found that, more often than not, when I tried to interpret the games, I seemed to disrupt whatever it was that was going on in Lesley's mind as she played. It seemed that my attempts at understanding needed to be largely kept to myself. Lesley was concentratedly trying to work out for herself the problem of how to hold herself together and contain what she had previously felt was uncontainable. My function seemed to be to enable her to do this without interrupting in any way the experience she was having at the time. It gradually became apparent that as Lesley became more and more immersed in these games, her fears of madness and hysterically losing control seemed to diminish, as did her suicidal wishes. I was aware of this through the change in the quality of her non-verbal communication, which became less desperate and fearful, as well as from my colleague who was working with her parents.

In time, snails and their shells, butterflies and chrysalises, anemones and their tentacles, fascinated Lesley. Themes of protection and safety preoccupied her. She talked about how butterflies emerge from chrysalises, as well as of caterpillars that stay inside their chrysalises too long and die. I was able to interpret that she did not know if she would be able to, or indeed would dare to, become a free butterfly again, as she had been before the rape. Although a part of her longed to recover and fly again, she was also aware of her strong wish to stay forever in the protected environment of her 'chrysalis'. The idea of a chrysalis seemed to symbolise her wish to bury herself within her mother, in a highly regressed and unhelpful manner.

The containment that Lesley so badly needed to experience through my therapeutic reverie and, indeed, the arguably necessary regression that took place in order to help Lesley recover, could clearly also become a tender trap for Lesley. The marble game that she played represented the dilemma she knew she faced. The delicacy of the balance between containment and entrapment did in fact become highly significant. Lesley would quite conceivably have become encapsulated in the way that Tustin described children with autism (1981). It is a popular concept, as well as clinically evident, that traumatic experiences can drive people mad, and produce severe regression.

From internal change to external behavioural change

There is a significant stage in all therapies where internal change needs to be translated into 'external' changes in actions and behaviour. Without these external changes, the work is incomplete. In some cases a very small issue can become the focus for this change. When I felt that Lesley was internally strong enough, I had to become more involved than was usual for me in her therapy with the practical management of her day-to-day life. The focus for this change was her continued difficulty to separate from her mother. Many months after the rape had taken place, she still required a great deal of encouragement and even some mild pressure to enable her to do many things she had done before the rape, such as to go to school on her own, or visit friends on her own. It had only been after a great deal of discussion and careful preparation in her parents' therapy that Lesley had been helped to dare to sleep on her own or let her mother even briefly out of her sight. Her parents had found it very difficult to risk her anger and distress. It was important that I remained alert to the early signs that Lesley was becoming more able to survive these tiny separations without them becoming a setback to her recovery, and communicate this to my colleague who worked with her parents. Regular discussions with my colleague helped us to judge as well as possible when each small step was attainable.

This separation issue came alive in the therapy after about ten months when Lesley started to become aware of other people who had suffered terribly, but had eventually been able to live a comparatively normal life again. In particular she identified with her kitten, Fluffy, who had been run over some time before the rape, and nearly died. The vet had wanted to put her down, but Lesley and her parents had tenderly nursed Fluffy, keeping her on a special blanket and syringe feeding her until she gradually recovered. The problem then was that Fluffy had become 'lazy' and would not do anything for herself. In the end, Lesley and her parents had refused to syringe feed her any more and Fluffy, after not eating for a short while, finally fed herself again. According to Lesley, Fluffy was then able to recover and became as lively and cheeky as she was before the accident. Lesley's wish to be 'lazy' was supported by the many attractions of staying in a safely encapsulated and regressed state, immersed within her mother's psyche. This clearly had to be resisted, as it had been with Fluffy, for both Lesley and her mother's sake.

The practical management of the case now became of critical importance as Lesley hesitatingly tried to take up her life again from where she had been before she was raped. This effort to help parents to change in their responses to a child, alongside the changes that emerge from within the child in therapy, is one of the reasons for offering therapeutic work with parents as a part of the treatment plan for the child. As indicated above, Lesley's parents now had to be actively encouraged through their therapist to resist Lesley's 'laziness' and help her to separate from her mother again. This came into the therapeutic relationship when I decided to insist that Lesley was quite capable of walking on her own from the parked car to the clinic (a distance of no more than 100 metres). Lesley's mother and father had become her slaves, terrified to resist her control in case she became severely distressed again. My insistence that Lesley was ready for this increased level of independence enabled her parents to start to take up this ordinary parenting skill again. Lesley was at first very angry with me for this interference, but the analogy of Fluffy's story helped us to work this through. In my opinion, these windows of opportunity to change actual behaviour, when built on evidence from the therapy that the time is ripe, need to be seized in order to promote development. They can be significant contributors to the process of change.

Interestingly, one of the important factors that seemed to be operating at this stage of the therapy was that I needed to be prepared to behave in a masterful, 'phallic' way and, with sensitivity, come firmly between Lesley and her mother to help them separate. Since Lesley's rape, normal male sexuality and assertiveness within the family had become almost totally synonymous with rape. Lesley's father's wish for an ordinary sexual relationship with his wife felt unacceptably entangled with the rapist's perverse sexuality and he experienced any mild attempt to be assertive with Lesley or his wife as a potentially dangerous assault on both of them. This was particularly difficult for him when Lesley and her mother were clearly becoming so unhealthily fused. From my experience of traumatised children and seriously ill children, I have often observed that this intense relationship between mother and child after the traumatic event is a natural reaction which most fathers can tolerate for a short time. When the mother and child are unable to allow the ordinary triangular relationship of the Oedipal stage to re-emerge, or the father is frightened of harming the child by reasserting the central importance of the sexual parental relationship to the family, marital problems can emerge which may lead to complete marital breakdown. The emotional well-being of the siblings is also at risk when the mother and traumatised child cannot allow for their needs as well.

Lesley stopped her twice-weekly therapy on her own insistence when she needed to move school and felt she wanted this to feel like a fresh start. She was unsure whether she would be able to manage without treatment, but was determined to try. We kept in touch for some time with monthly consultations and then more occasional consultations, because of the continuing need to reintegrate the reality of the trauma as Lesley matured. These memories made her very serious and sad, but they no longer incapacitated her. Thinking in terms of there being a season for all things, this seemed to indicate that the process of mourning what had once been (her life before the rape) had started to take place.

Derek

The violent and traumatic circumstances which led to 9-year-old Derek being adopted – his mother's murder by her partner when he was 2 and a half – was a taboo subject in his new family. Indeed, it was not easy for his adoptive parents to accept that there might be any connection between this and the alarming behaviour that had prompted their request for help. They were worried that Derek seemed to keep putting his life at risk – for example, by jumping out of first-floor windows, or cycling recklessly along a busy road close to their home. They said that he seemed to believe that he was like a cat with nine lives.

The murder had taken place over six years before I saw Derek for twice-weekly therapy, and during this time he had needed to erect very strong defences in order to survive. The manic omnipotence of his reckless behaviour had become the only way that he could cope with underlying feelings of extreme paralysing helplessness. In the course of his therapy, I became convinced that he had either seen the murder, or at least seen all the events leading up to it. He had been a helpless, terrified bystander.

Like Lesley, Derek also avoided any close relationships, so that his warm, adoptive parents found that he kept slipping through their fingers despite their efforts to keep a careful eye on him. In fact, he engendered a mildly neglectful attitude in all the adults around him, although they were simultaneously aware of how desperately he needed to be taken in hand and kept safe. He was generally thought of as a loveable little boy, but he could not accept love and affection other than on a very superficial level. Although I do not wish to go into detail about these processes in the context of this chapter, his adoptive parents' 'neglectfulness' as well as mine at times in the transference, were probably powerful transferential communications of aspects of his early relationships with his mother and her partner. (There is a fuller discussion of the therapeutic relationship with children who have been severely traumatised and are subsequently fostered and/or adopted in Chapter 6.)

It is very possible that Derek experienced neglect and witnessed violence between his mother and her partner before the murder took place, although the transference relationship also indicated that he had been a loved child at other times. There was a very strong pull towards acting out neglectful and harmful experiences in the transference as well as in his adoptive parents' care of him in his day-to-day life. This happened despite our all being very aware of how uncannily this seemed to keep happening. The unconscious power of the compulsion to repeat traumatic experiences in the present needs to be constantly borne in mind when working with traumatised patients. This can happen within the network of professionals working with the patient, as well as in their everyday and therapeutic relationships.

It was clear to me from Derek's first consultation that there was a great deal of confusion between fantasies about what had happened to his parents and dim memories of what he had actually witnessed. During this consultation, he played with a fire engine, saying it was on the way to a fire that had been started deliberately to kill some people. The fire engine could not get there because someone had 'cut the wire' and it had broken down. He felt sorry for the people who died in the fire. They needed help but it did not come. He moved from this fantasy play to what he claimed was an actual experience of seeing two trains crash into each other. He said that he had seen them from a railway bridge heading for each other, but could not do anything to stop them. The two drivers were killed, but the passengers managed to jump out of the windows of the train. I was rather stunned by the clarity of this account. It seemed to be a screen memory of the violent crash of his mother and her partner, and Derek's narrow escape. I said that he seemed to be telling me about something awful that he had seen happen, and not been able to stop. He agreed with me.

Derek and I were aware from the start that we were talking about a real traumatic experience, as well as his terrifying fantasies and confusing memories surrounding it. However, there was a serious difficulty in ever talking with him about what was known about the reasons for his adoption. In the early days of his adoption, Derek's adoptive parents had struggled to understand what Derek had been through and had taken the courageous step of visiting Derek's mother's partner in prison. He had pleaded guilty to murder and from their account of this meeting, it seemed to have been a crime of passion. Derek had not been directly in danger of attack and had been found wandering the streets. This had led to the discovery of the murder. Derek's adoptive parents felt that he did not yet need to know what had actually happened to his birth parents, although they knew that as he grew older they would probably need to find a way to tell him the truth. This left me with my hands rather tied when material clearly linked to the murder emerged in the therapy. As with Lesley, the question of what needed to be put into words and what needed (for the present) to stay at a non-verbal level was a constant preoccupation in Derek's therapy, as well as in the work that his parents undertook with a colleague.

During the first year of twice-weekly therapy, there was a consistent pattern of one intense session full of warmth and pain, being followed by many sessions of determined withdrawal – a pattern which could be described as typical of a child with an ambivalent/disorganised attachment pattern (Solomon and George 1999). The experience of a warm relationship was particularly painful for Derek to bear. His fantasy play often concerned 'rescuers' who suddenly turned into violent aggressors in a Jekyll and Hyde fashion. On a transference level, this may well have been a reflection of his experience with his mother and her partner – that they were sometimes loving, but then suddenly, incomprehensibly, extremely frightening for him. Derek felt that I was like this towards him, particularly during the gaps between sessions and holiday times. While this partly reflected the transference, it also related to our present relationship in which he was struggling with whether he dared to allow more tender feelings of closeness to emerge between us. His experience of my attempts to contain him both drew him towards me and terrified him. Despite this conflict, he nevertheless became much more contained generally and stopped stealing and behaving dangerously. As some of his defences melted, he was able to allow himself to return more often to a closer relationship with me.

The endless fall

Derek managed well during the second summer break in therapy and was openly glad to see me again. The recognition of this pleasure, however, proved to be the final straw that made many of Derek's defences collapse. Suddenly the terror and devastation within him were laid bare as he became terribly vulnerable and deeply, frighteningly depressed. For many weeks he either sat in severely broody silence during the sessions, or he viciously attacked any half-hearted attempts he managed at drawing or making models. Derek would rip at his drawings with a penknife or tear them apart with his hands. Occasionally, his drawings gave me some insight into what he was experiencing inside the 'black hole' that he felt he was endlessly falling into. In one such drawing, a man was in mid-air having been pushed off the edge of a chasm and shot as he fell. At the bottom of the chasm there were sharks waiting to eat him. The man cried out 'Help, don't kill me!' Superman came along and provided a trampoline so that the man could bounce back out of the chasm before the sharks got him. The superman figure was pathetically unbelievable and more in keeping with desperate, manic wish-fulfilment than any genuine resolution of his central anxiety. Regretfully, because Derek and Lesley were seen so many years ago, I no longer have the drawings that they did in therapy, although they remain vivid in my mind.

Derek spent many sessions binding his hands and arms so thickly with Sellotape that it became like a plaster cast. He got through roll after roll of Sellotape and became hooked on what he called 'escaping' from the Sellotape 'just in time' for the end of the session. As well as the ever-present theme of escape from danger in his play, there was a clear sado-masochistic sexual excitement in this binding. He sometimes bound his arm so tightly that he restricted the blood supply to his fingers. Getting out of the Sellotape was also most alarming, as he would hack at it with scissors or a penknife. I often had to intervene to stop him from hurting himself when he was locked in this compulsive behaviour.

Khan and Masud (1979a) describe sexual perversity as being a means of splitting off mental pain. This was certainly true for Derek. He used this binding not only as a means of holding himself together when he feared he would fall apart (Bick 1968), but also as a way of eroticising and holding in the violent explosion of pain that he felt was so imminent. Throughout a large part of this distressing time I found that there was absolutely nothing I could usefully interpret to Derek, as words literally failed me. I felt shocked and battered by the sessions, which had become an ordeal for both of us. There were many interpretations that could have been made in terms of his identifications with his murdered mother or murderer 'father figure'. However, I felt that it was more important at this point in the therapy for Derek and I to live through and survive the experience we were having. I restricted myself to occasional comments along these lines. My therapeutic reverie was full of awful images and thoughts about what he had probably witnessed and his extreme terror. I was also full of sadness to witness his current painful and hopeless depression and not be able to somehow magically take it away from him. This could have been the result of his projection into me of his magical wishes as a toddler to stop the violence that he saw between his mother and her partner.

Although the wordless experience was a very different one to that which I had with Lesley, due to the violent feelings that Derek was struggling with, my state of mind seemed to need to be similarly resolute and patient, awaiting the time when we would emerge from this awful period. This seemed to be the only way that I could contain his extreme anxieties. I had to witness the dreadful time he was going through and be aware of the dangers to him and to me as a bystander, without being able to 'do' anything about it.

The fact that I allowed him to bring his penknife to the room intrigues me after all these years. I don't know that I would allow it now – but of course, allowing or not allowing is often not a choice as the therapist can suddenly find him or herself in the room with a patient who is armed in this way. But Derek consistently bought the knife and I don't seem to have tried to stop him. I now wonder whether this was related to the 'neglectfulness' that I have already referred to, which kept being acted out in the transference. It became rather too concrete an example of the way in which I came to experience the helplessness that Derek had felt when witnessing the violence between his mother and her partner.

The safe landing

The hell that Derek was going through first showed signs of abating when he struggled through blizzards to the clinic for his session, arriving an hour late. Fortunately (with the pressure to repeat 'neglectful' transferences very much on my mind) I had also managed to arrive, very late, for his appointment. This seemed to wordlessly confirm how important the therapeutic relationship was to both us, despite the awfulness of what it was trying to contain. Derek had often in the past been able to be wistfully in touch with the tenderness within him when he enjoyed the view from my window. For the first time since his depression had begun (three months earlier), he was able to do this again and felt touched by the snow scene. He pointed it out to me and said it was as if we were the only two survivors in a sea of snow. I risked the comment that he seemed to be able to feel close to me again for the first time for months, without being too terrified. I was very struck by the fact that there were now two survivors in his mind, not just himself as the sole survivor of an internal apocalypse.

At first he predictably scornfully rubbished this with his words, but his body language and demeanour suggested that he was nevertheless more amenable than he had been since he had become so depressed. So I decided to try to expand, step by step, on my previous interpretation. With each extra bit of interpretation, I watched carefully to see if Derek could take in what I was saying. I started by saying how terrifyingly painful it was for Derek to feel close and tender towards me, because he was so afraid of being hurt by this closeness. I then added that he always seemed to have to destroy the experience, possibly because it felt much safer to stay away. When he seemed able to listen to this, I linked these defences to the abrupt and not understood loss of his birth parents and my belief, as borne out by the transference relationship, that he had felt loved by his parents. He felt that he had lost this love suddenly, in a horrifying way. As he was still listening, I said that he now seemed to feel that he dared not trust in or feel love for anyone else again. Derek was able to take in all this interpretation, which is of the kind in which I often feel as if I am 'tiptoeing' up to the patient with my words. He blinked back some tears and this was possibly an early sign of the process of very delayed mourning for the loss of his birth parents coming into play.

On looking back on this experience in therapy, I think that the shared gazing at the snow scene was an example of a moment-of-meeting between us (Stern *et al.* 1998). It came in the midst of an otherwise barren expanse of therapy in which very little felt salvageable. By risking saying what I did, I was taking advantage of what I perceived to be a window in his defences following the moment-of-meeting, through which I just might be able to reach him. Metaphorically, I effectively took a big step towards him and in this way exposed my personal self, more than was usual between us. The big step was actually made up of several little steps. The step-by-step nature of the interpretation itself was the kind I quite often find myself using when it is hard to judge how much or how little to share of my understanding of what is happening in therapy. Significantly, what was said was from the heart and I think received by his heart, which was why it was so moving for both of us.

Derek's way out of the abyss he felt himself trapped in was a tortuous one, vividly illustrated by the mazes full of dead ends which now fascinated him. He spent many sessions drawing complicated mazes, which I had to find my way out of. I, in turn, had to draw mazes for him to do. His renewed capacity to think was a great relief to him. In addition to the contributions of the therapeutic processes that I have already described, I would now conceptualise this change by hypothesising that what felt at the time to him (and me) as if his brain had started to work, was in fact a reality – his brain *had* started to work, possibly with a renewed growth spurt in the right hemisphere in response to the experiences of therapy (Schore 2002). We now know that for the brain to grow, it needs to have experiences; if it does not, it atrophies in what is effectively a kind of neural pruning. However, as well as new experiences, presumably the ordinary physical growth processes of childhood and the sudden much bigger growth of puberty and adolescence are also times when the brain has the potential to grow (Schore 2002).

It is not out of the question to hypothesise that the experiences of being listened to and understood that are so fundamental to the therapeutic process are the kinds of experiences that might promote brain growth. In this new parallel universe of brain and mind, it is again stating the obvious to remember that the brain is the organ of the mind. Observing the mind grow, as we often do in therapy, may quite realistically be an external counterpart of the growth of the brain. The specific contribution of psychoanalysis to this process is the understanding that it offers of the very complex and disturbing communications from the patient to the listening psychotherapist. This lends a particular quality to the listening that takes place, as well as to the words that are used within each unique patient-therapist dyad.

As with Lesley, after some time Derek and I reached a crucial point where a pragmatic intervention on my part seemed necessary. He was in such obvious internal chaos at times that he felt quite unable to sort out what was 'good' within him from what was 'bad'. I proposed that I would try to help him to find his way. This quite literally involved preventing him from destroying the good drawings and models that he had made when he was with me. I took them and looked after them, but allowed him access to them as long as he did not start destroying them again. Although initially bemused by this, Derek responded gratefully and seemed to confirm that my managerial hunch was right, by starting to produce many drawings on the theme of planes and rockets landing safely, but gingerly, on firm ground. The fear of endless falling, which had been Derek's worst fear, appeared to have been finally met by his finding a safe place to land.

Our games progressed (on his instigation) to playing 'dots' in which a grid of dots on paper are joined together by the players taking turns to join them up. He suddenly started to see swastikas and the sign of the Cross in the line patterns. This theme of good and evil crosses continued to surprise him by appearing out of the blue in his drawings and doodles. We were now able to talk about what he identified as the dangerous Nazi, hating part of his personality that could only bring him grief, if it got out of hand, and the Christian, loving side of him that he needed to mobilise to help himself keep out of trouble, at the very least. This is a good illustration of the need to help patients to recognise their strengths and weaknesses and to use conscious control to curb those weaknesses. It was important that Derek could recognise the shadow side, or as he saw it, the 'Nazi' side of himself. As he emerged from his depression, he seemed to know himself better, and in quite an adult way to have become able to struggle with the duality within him. He gradually became able to distinguish for himself between the useful remains from the internal holocaust, which he could build on, and the perverted debris that led to misery. He could now identify what he felt to be the enemy within him, and actively fight it. Derek gradually became more able to trust in others to help him. This was symbolised by a change in the way he used the Sellotape. He no longer used it to bind himself, but instead used it to make a kind of hammock seat across the wooden arms of the chair, which could take his weight.

Derek stopped therapy before I felt it was really wise, mostly due to external circumstances. By this point, he was able to function much better in school and he continued not to put himself into dangerous situations or to steal. Further help was needed during his adolescence and I do not know if and when his adoptive parents told him fully about his past. We had gone some of the way towards helping him to digest his traumatic past, but there was still, not surprisingly, a lot more help required. At least stopping as we did, on a positive note when he felt well and his parents were pleased with his progress, allowed him to feel more able to return to the clinic at a later stage for further help. There is a fuller discussion of the ending of therapy in general later in this book (see Chapter 8).

The problem with words . . .

There were silences and quiet periods of many different qualities and contents in the course of Lesley's and Derek's therapy. Winnicott (1958) draws attention to the developmental importance of 'being alone in the presence of someone' which is essentially a quiet and peaceful experience. He stresses the creative value of the capacity to be alone, which he clearly differentiates from pathological regression or withdrawal. Balint (1968) develops this concept when he describes in the treatment of some adult patients 'a fault within him, a fault that must be put right' (p. 21). He talks of the therapeutic task of healing the 'basic fault' as 'inactivating the basic fault by creating conditions in which it can heal itself'. Balint also emphasises the need for 'undisturbed peace, experiment and experience' in creating these conditions. By inference, while remaining very alert to the patient, these are times when the therapist also needs to strive for a peacefulness and stillness within – a state of mind that is at times not far removed from a meditative state.

During the early stages of therapy, verbal interpretations disrupted and interfered with the quiet therapeutic process that Lesley and Derek seemed to be trying to experience within the present relationship with me. Experiencing this process, rather than talking about its content, seemed to be what helped them most. The process was aided by my therapeutic reverie that I now understand as being separate from the way in which events and relationships from the past came into the transference relationship. For example, when Lesley experienced me as the cause of all of her distress and hated me for this, in the transference I had become the man who raped her. However, often simultaneously, she also experienced me as someone who in the present relationship could bear to stay with her despite her emotional untouchableness. During this time she was often in my thoughts and in fact felt very 'present' to me because of this. Derek was also in my thoughts a great deal, but it was harder to hold onto the compassionate side of this therapeutic reverie as he had such a potential for becoming violent. He was uncomfortable to have 'in my pocket' as he projected such violent images into me – much more than Lesley did.

In the light of the physicality that is implied by the neuro-scientific explorations of two minds interacting, my sense of literally 'carrying' patients around with me when they are going through very difficult phases in therapy no longer feels as far-fetched as it did (Schore 2002). Just as the therapeutic interaction may well physically affect the patient's brain and neuro-chemical systems, with the parasympathetic system becoming more active when there are calming influences, so too is the therapist's body affected by the feelings and experiences received and shared within each patient-therapist dyad.

This whole process illustrates the quiet and slowly incremental aspect of therapeutic change. This built up gradually for Lesley and Derek resulting for both of them in communication in words, from me, which lead to the 'noisier' kind of change that I have referred to before. For Lesley, this emerged through her play with the wooden houses and marbles. In Derek's treatment, we reached a moment-of-meeting on a snowy day, after which he slowly started to come out of his deeply depressed state.

Part of the function of the quiet times in Lesley and Derek's therapies seemed to be to prepare the ground for when they became able to play in a free and creative way, around the issues that were central to their silent preoccupations and projections into me. The sense of therapy facilitating the creation of this transitional space that allows for the free expression in play form of such dire thoughts and feelings, is central to my ideas about how therapeutic change comes about. There seems to be a 'transitional' phase in treatment when there is a potential for change, before the change itself can clearly be seen to be taking place. This reminds me of Stern's (1985) concept of the 'sense of emergent self' which precedes the quantum leap to the next stage of sense of self.

Psychoanalytically informed 'actions' are also beyond words, and particularly important in work with children and young people. My involvement with trying to help Lesley to let go of her mother and become more independent, and my decision to help Derek sort out the 'good' from the 'bad' drawings, were psychoanalytic actions which bought about change. In the context of helping traumatised patients to feel less frightened, my actions helped them to face, in a small but significant way, something that they both felt very frightened of – for Lesley, daring to separate, and for Derek, the devastation of his life following the murder of his mother. Having the courage to face, even in such a diluted dose, something linked with their trauma was facilitated by the quality of companionship in the present relationship. It was hard to do, but having done it, both children started to feel stronger within.

Over time, I did gradually manage to communicate to Lesley and Derek many of the thoughts and feelings that were projected into me. This only occurred when I felt that they were strong enough to bear it. However, some of the vivid scenes of rape and murder that they had filled me with I felt had to stay within me, as an essential part of my therapeutic function. They were both aware that when they were older they could need more therapy. I envisaged that, with greater maturity, they might be more able consciously to acknowledge and talk about what had happened to them. But at the time of their therapy, I felt that this would be more than they could bear. However, they knew that I 'knew' and at the time this appeared to be 'good enough'.

Deciphering and disentangling the strands of the total therapeutic relationship relies on the recognition that it must be the therapist's professional responsibility to keep sorting out which parts of his or her total response to the patient relate to the transference relationship, the present relationship, or to aspects of the therapist's personality, history and ways of relating that are a part of his or her non-professional life. This will always be a difficult area because its discussion is somewhat revealing of the therapist's personality, and carries the risk of blurring professional and personal boundaries. Training psychoanalysis, as well as ongoing personal analysis or therapy after training, help the therapist to maintain this sorting process, as do supervision and the process of discussing work with colleagues. The next chapter illustrates how complicated this process can be.

Chapter 3

Variations on the theme of transference and counter-transference[1]

Some patients enter therapy with an intensity of feeling and need that touches the therapist much more deeply and on a more personal level than do others. This can and should raise questions in the psychotherapist's mind about what this intensity of feeling means. There can be a legitimate concern that the response is part of an unprofessional and ultimately unhelpful emotional over-involvement with the patient. This may be due to some neurotic conflict within the therapist which the patient unwittingly fits into. In the best interests of the patient, the therapist must therefore always be prepared to think long and hard about such emotional responses, privately and in discussion with colleagues.

But when it becomes sufficiently likely that this is *not* a neurotic response on the psychotherapist's part, he or she is left with a phenomenon that is very clearly related to the patient, which the psychotherapist then comes to live with during the course of the therapy. In such cases there is a great deal to be learnt about transference and counter-transference, because subtleties which are often difficult to decipher in other therapies are here written large. This chapter is about a patient who affected me in this way.

Freud's discovery of the counter-transference (Freud 1910) and the realisation of its great importance for psychoanalytic work led to the establishment of training analysis as essential in all psychoanalytic training. Racker (1957), points out how puzzling it was that so little attention was nevertheless paid to counter-transference in the literature for nearly 40 years. It was as if, having accorded the analyst's feelings such central significance, they were swiftly tidied away into the private area of training analysis, almost as if they were too revealing of the humanity and personality of the

---

1 Much of this chapter was originally published in 1989 as 'Variations on the theme of transference and counter-transference in the treatment of a ten year old boy', *Journal of Child Psychotherapy*, 15(2): 85–102. In this chapter I have clarified my thinking from the original paper and added some new thoughts in the context of the subject matter of the book.

apist or psychoanalyst to be comfortably out in the open. And
o doubt that discussion of counter-transference issues does make
herapists personally and professionally vulnerable, whether this
lace in the privacy of personal supervision or in a seminar or group
.

There have been two distinct attitudes towards counter-transference
(Kernberg 1975). According to Kernberg the first, which he terms the
'classical' view, argues that counter-transference reflects neurotic conflicts
in the psychotherapist and is effectively a problem which must be overcome – in rather the same way as transference was originally regarded.
The second, which he terms the 'totalistic' view, regards counter-
transference as consisting of the total emotional reaction of the therapist
to the patient. Here, counter-transference is regarded as more of a blessing,
and one of the main therapeutic tools that is used to bring about understanding. Within the total counter-transference response it is possible to
distinguish various strands of response from the psychotherapist. In this
chapter I hope to illustrate, in particular, the strands that come from
different types of projective identification, the impact of projection itself
and the function of the present relationship alongside this.

The classical view of counter-transference would argue that the totalistic
view is too broad and potentially shifts the therapist from a valuable
neutral position, opening the way for the possibly dangerous intrusion of
the psychotherapist's personality into the patient's treatment. There is
already inevitably somewhat of an imbalance of power within the ordinary
psychotherapeutic relationship. If the psychotherapist is not sufficiently
aware of maintaining a professionalism which is often characterised as
holding a 'neutral' position, there can be ethical issues raised because
acceptable boundaries are more likely to be breached (McFarland Solomon
and Twyman 2003). A willingness in the psychotherapist to scrutinise the
counter-transference helps to address these very serious issues.

Freud claimed that 'neutrality does not mean loss of spontaneity, of
the natural warmth of the analyst' and that 'listless indifference on the
analyst's part may in itself bring about resistance in the patient' (Meng
and Freud 1963). I think that this is particularly true when working with
children and young people where the psychotherapist inevitably has to be
more present and interactive with the external world, inside and outside
the therapy room, than with adult patients. For example, the practical
need to maintain reasonable boundaries within the session, particularly
when a child is behaving violently or dangerously, indicates very clearly
what the therapist as a person can tolerate, or feels is safe or dangerous
for the patient. Long periods in some therapies can be spent with the
patients testing out the resilience of these limits again and again – as
with John in this chapter and Nicky in the next. The setting and
environment in which child and adolescent psychotherapy takes place

therefore takes on a much greater therapeutic significance than in most adult therapies.

Above all, the human reactivity of the psychotherapist's face and body language is constantly evident to the child and adolescent patient. In the past I think that I tried too hard to restrain this visual and auditory evidence and probably became rather stilted in my way of being with my patients. This question of how to 'be yourself' with patients is very difficult and owes much to the accumulation of clinical experience. It cannot be taught, but it can be facilitated as a live process within the psychotherapist that originates in training, is worked through privately in training analysis and is facilitated by wise supervision. This process needs to be alive and growing throughout the psychotherapist's working life and is central to thinking about how the psychotherapist's 'personal signature' inevitably gives its particular flavour and uniqueness to each therapeutic couple (Tronick 2001).

While there may be a consensus of opinion about how to understand a particular dynamic in a therapy, together with a consensus on the kind of response that is required for this understanding, the individual way in which the *communication itself* takes place within the therapy will depend utterly on the particular patient-therapist couple. Psychotherapists who have had more than one experience of training or personal therapy confirm what common sense tells us: that psychotherapy with one therapist is not at all the same as having therapy with another. It is experientially different even if at times very similar things have actually been said.

However, therapists who are similarly open to receiving the verbal and non-verbal communications of the patient are likely to receive and try to process similar words and projections from the same patient. As Kernberg helpfully puts it 'given reasonably well-adjusted therapists, all hypothetically dealing with the same severely regressed and disorganised patient, their counter-transference reactions will be somewhat similar – reflecting the patient's problems much more than any specific problem of the analyst's past'. Heimann and Racker both emphasised that this counter-transference reaction is not only one of the most important therapeutic tools, but is also an instrument of research into the patient's unconscious (Heimann 1950; Racker 1957).

The refinement of psychoanalytic thinking about projection and projective identification in particular have contributed enormously to our understanding of the mechanisms and processes involved in everyday communication of emotions throughout life. Parent-infant observation, which is central to psychoanalytic training, provides endless illustrations of these ordinary processes as they first occur, between parents and pre-verbal babies. These concepts have greatly illuminated what goes on in the therapy room between patient and therapist, particularly at a non-verbal level. Those feelings experienced by the analyst, which in the past might have given rise to some uneasiness about intrusions of the analyst's personality into the treatment, can now be scrutinised as possibly being the result of primitive non-verbal communications from the patient to the psychotherapist.

Positive counter-transference: John

To illustrate these issues, I would like to describe a powerful experience in therapy, with a boy I shall call John, who was 10 at the start of his treatment. He was seen three times weekly in a residential therapeutic unit, which I will describe in more detail in the next chapter. The unit worked with children who had at least one parent who was committed to the child and the aim was to help the child to live at home at the end of treatment. John was referred to the unit because of his abusiveness and violence to other children, his very low self-esteem (he often said 'I'm just a load of shit') and his complete inability to cope in a classroom, despite his above-average intelligence. He had been on the 'at risk' register since he was a toddler and had had short periods in foster care because at times his mother became violent towards him and his father was unable to stop her. His mother had some mental health problems and his father had been seriously ill and bedridden for two years. A colleague in the residential setting worked with John's parents throughout his placement. He went home regularly and it was hoped that he would be able to live at home again when he went to secondary school.

In discussions at the time of his referral for therapy, I did not hear anyone say anything good about John, to the extent that I awaited the first session with some trepidation. This must have contributed to my complete surprise at the positive emotional impact he made on me. He was vulnerable and subdued. He was also full of sadness and loss regarding his ill father. He knew that he quite deliberately tried to avoid showing anger and upset to his mum, as he was aware that she could not cope with this and could resort to hitting him in her frustration. There was a painful, intense quality to the contact throughout the session. I was taken aback at the end of the session when John said, 'You needn't have got all those toys out for me after all' – he had barely used them and had mainly talked – 'but thank you anyway.' He was genuinely grateful for the time and attention he had had with me. After the session, I commented in my notes 'Strong positive transference – as if he feels he's found what he needs and immediately starts to use it'.

John's use of me felt as instinctive as a newborn baby going straight to the breast. He was rather like someone who has struggled to carry a heavy load for a long while, and suddenly sees a place where he or she can put it down. John immediately started to make use of me as someone who was available to become a container for his feelings, thoughts and fantasies (Bion 1962b). He lost no time at all in using our sessions to this end.

It is important that I clarify *what* aspects of himself John felt he could project into me and safely leave there, for I rapidly became aware of a perplexing aspect to our relationship. We spent the first six months of his therapy involved in what I can only describe as a kind of mutual adoration, which made me feel extremely uneasy. As well as projecting strong feelings of love, loss and sadness into me, he also treated me as if I was a very precious, goddess-like figure to him. Outside his sessions he continued to be foul-mouthed. However, he would be appalled if he inadvertently swore when with me, and had great difficulty being in touch with any anger he felt towards me. I frequently interpreted this in terms of his intense fear that I would reject him or even attack him as his mum had, but this did not resonate with what he was actually experiencing at the time. However much I could see that this image of me was idealised and full of fear of rejection, it seemed that I had to stick with what he was consciously feeling, however unreal it felt to me, if I was to start to understand what was going on within him. His primary need was that I understand *his* view of the relationship, and not insist that he take mine.

From the start of the therapy I had been aware of the intense love John felt for his mum, despite her attacks on him. This was not defensive; it was real and powerfully contributed to the passionate nature of their relationship. I struggled to accept this paradox, as I found it hard to understand intellectually. The evidence for the reality that she, and John's father, were both at times able to be good parents to John was to be seen in a number of areas. For example, John was able to play creatively on his own, displaying a rich fantasy life, and he experienced great pleasure in art and music, which he had absorbed from his parents. His play often involved loving behaviour between people, which combined with his attitude towards me convinced me that he must have been, and still was, a much loved child. It felt as if he had received good enough parenting for a reasonable amount of his childhood, but that it had been patchy.

The problem lay with the dark side of this passionate love that could rapidly become violent. I was therefore very concerned about the split that existed in the therapy. My thinking led me to believe that the unexpressed dark side of John's love, if not expressed in the sessions, would remain unavailable to change. I also thought it likely that the split within him contributed to his aggression towards the other children and adults in the unit. However, to my surprise, after a few months, when I enquired about his progress within the therapeutic unit I was told that he was felt to be 'getting better'. This made me think that the positive transference/counter-transference relationship must be serving some function that as yet I did not understand.

Looking back on this time in John's therapy, I feel certain that this experience belonged to the transference relationship and not the present relationship. This is because the whole experience felt so weird to me at the time, and not ego-syntonic in the way that a present relationship tends to feel. I was aware of something projected into me that felt rather alien and yet which I needed to have reside within me, in order that I gradually came to understand it.

Even more perturbing than John's idealising and 'precious' response to me was my response to him. From the first session I felt that I was working with a wonderful, creative child. I wondered what on earth had happened to the negative transference that was bound to exist somewhere, even if I was not in touch with it at the time. While remaining aware that hostile feelings would eventually have to enter into the therapy, all that I could do was wait until the time felt right to John.

In the meantime, I was at least starting to understand within my therapeutic reverie about John why this should be the case. Although I never expressed my very positive feelings towards him, he needed to know from his ongoing experience with me how completely accepted and 'loved' in a therapeutic sense he was by me before he would ever risk any hatred or aggression towards me. Particularly because this was happening right at the start of his treatment and had the quality of 'love being blind', I felt that it was the result of a particular form of projective identification, described by Ogden (1979), in which a *feeling was induced* in me as a result of a projection from my patient. Rather than making me feel terribly frightened and rejected as John himself had felt, he seemed to be inducing in me the way his mother felt about him when she was loving towards him. This experience was what helped me to understand the passion of her love for him, which was essential if I was also to understand how terrible was her hatred of him. Carpy (1989) writes about the tolerance of this kind of projective identification and its significance in the counter-transference experience.

Here we get to another uncomfortable experience in the counter-transference. I cannot get away from the fact that what I felt for John was a form of love. Why should I feel uncomfortable about this? Certainly it relates to the need to be ever aware of professional boundaries, as discussed above. But I think it also relates to something within the psychoanalytic culture which is very uncomfortable with the expression of feelings related to love. Psychoanalytic thinking is perfectly comfortable with the projection of hatred, anger, envy, jealousy – all the negative aspects of human nature. Yet at the same time, why should love, warmth, caring and gratitude not also be powerfully experienced within the total therapeutic relationship? Many therapists talk privately of being very fond of particular patients, of missing them and finding it painful when the therapy ends. A capacity to love is one of the most important signs of emotional health. It is nevertheless very difficult to think about within the therapeutic relationship, although it may be very present within the therapeutic reverie at various phases in the treatment.

The reality of John's past traumatic beatings, and the cruelty that he had received from somebody who also loved him, needed to be experienced within the transference relationship. It seemed that he needed a long period of time securely embedded in the positive transference/counter-transference process before we could start to experience the dark side of his nature within his therapy. As with Lesley and Derek, there seemed to be a 'season', a right time, for these feelings to emerge.

At the phase in therapy when I was trying to understand my positive counter-transference, an observation of a newborn baby was fortuitously presented at the parent-baby observation seminar group that I led. The observer noted that the mother 'gazed at the baby at the breast all the time, even if he didn't look at her'. This very talkative mother was completely quiet and totally absorbed in her baby during feeding, and the adults around her all naturally followed her cue and were silent – in the observer's words, 'as if in the presence of a hallowed couple'. The observer felt that when in this state of mind, nothing else in the world existed for the mother, apart from the baby. Anecdotal evidence and everyday experience tend to confirm that, particularly with very young babies, the mother and father spend an enormous amount of time gazing in rapture at their offspring. To an outsider this may seem rather extreme. But this experience for the baby is the foundation of healthy narcissism and feeling loved, and a central component of primary parental preoccupation (developing Winnicott's concept and making it inclusive), without which a sound sense of self cannot develop (Winnicott 1956).

My patient needed to reach back to this experience, which I feel sure he had had in the past and still had at times in the present, in order to feel secure enough to face the dreadful shattering of this intimacy which occurred when his mother, apparently out of the blue, attacked him. I came to understand that my embarrassment at the intensity of my feelings towards John related to my knowledge that, as with mother and newborn baby, they seemed somewhat 'over the top' when viewed from 'outside' the therapeutic relationship but were nevertheless compelling when experienced from within that relationship. While it is often very hard to see what other parents find so adorable in *their* babies, it is always very clear to a parent what is adorable in their own.

Some patients need their therapists to be available to this intensity of *positive* experience with them. In such circumstances, it could be a defensive manoeuvre within the counter-transference if the therapist was unable to tolerate this unusual experience and try to understand it. Carpy helpfully discusses this dynamic by suggesting that some inevitable and partial acting out by the therapist may allow the patient 'to see consciously or uncon-sciously, that she is affecting the analyst and inducing strong feelings in him, and it allows her to observe him attempting to deal with these feelings' (1989: 292).

The shattering of intimacy

The first direct contact I had with John's stormier feelings did not come until we had been meeting for five months. He was playing with the animals, and small figures in the sand. He made a secret cave which the 'King' had visited in the past. The cave was now filled with hidden treasure and guarded by more animals. In another part of the sandpit, a man had been buried alive. I felt that the play symbolised secret hidden memories of John's father, before he fell ill. I had learnt through his therapy that John's father had been a playful man who enjoyed making things with his son. I said to John that I thought his play related to very special memories of his dad before his illness (the buried alive man) which were like hidden treasure. John agreed that he did have good memories. I then ventured to suggest, very tentatively, that there were also bad memories – of his mum and dad fighting, in particular. I linked this to the ferocious, blood-curdling fights that often went on between the male and female animals in his play.

At first he accepted all this, then suddenly he erupted. He said, 'How do you know all this? Pauline [the parent's worker] is not meant to tell you. It's gone, it's past. You're not meant to know.' He was very upset and angry, as if he felt all his past wounds were now very public knowledge. I replied, 'I do know about the rows your parents have and we've talked about your mum hitting you before now, but I actually don't know that much. You suddenly seem to think that I know much more than I do.' I was actually very surprised by his reaction to what I had said. John didn't believe me. He accused me of lying to him and demanded to know how I knew about the fights. I realised that by my use of the word 'fighting' instead of 'arguing', I had triggered a lot of very painful and guilt-ridden memories of violence between the parents, particularly of when John and his mum had hit his ill father in fury and frustration during the strains the illness added to the family. I felt terrible, as if I had clumsily and unnecessarily wounded him – which I possibly had. With hindsight this was one of those technical mistakes from which a lot can be learnt, but that are nevertheless regretted greatly at the time (Casement 2002). I said, 'John, I didn't actually mean "fighting" as in hitting each other, although that is clearly how you heard me. Now all sorts of unwanted memories and feelings seem to be suddenly here.' To which John replied, 'I don't want to remember them. I just want to forget. I was doing really well, getting much better and now you've spoilt it all. This is the worst day of my life – now everything's ruined.'

John managed to stay with me until the end of the session and much to his credit his distress was kept within the relationship with me and did not spill over into the rest of his day. I also felt upset during the session, and had great difficulty restraining myself from comforting him as I would one of my own children and telling him how sorry I was to have hurt him. If I had done so, this of course would have been the breaking of a boundary;

but my awareness of this strong wish kept me in touch with the way his mother may well have felt when she had recovered her thinking after having attacked John. My inadvertent use of words had destroyed his previous feelings of intimacy with me, and from this time on the mutual adoration started to decline.

The rapid change from intimacy to frightening exposure and danger that John suddenly felt, which made him furious with me as well as frightened of me, gave me a valuable insight into the way in which his relationship with his mother could fluctuate wildly. It was bewildering and shatteringly painful. The stark contrast between Winnicott's concept of gradual disillusionment following ordinary primary maternal preoccupation (Winnicott 1956) and what seems to have been John's experience of a shattered intimacy, was very striking.

Maternal stress with young babies

John's relationship and experience with his mother was of a sublime, rich intimacy that would unaccountably shatter into a horrifying, nightmarish parody of what had been. This militated against John being able to bring together the good and bad experiences in his mind. Quite the contrary, it reinforced a very powerful split in which his memories and knowledge of good experiences had to be protected from annihilation by the bad experiences (Klein 1946). In effect, when all was well with his mum, he had no awareness at all of the dark side of the relationship; and when he was in his nightmare world, he had no awareness of the other creative and loving world. His therapy was illustrative of that split in his mind.

Parent-infant observation offers many illuminating examples of the powerful impact a baby has on a family. The first baby in particular makes extraordinary demands on the mother's ability to adjust and grow during a period of great internal and external change. What carries her through this period of complete dedication of herself to the baby is her love of her child, which enables her to bear with the times when she also hates the seemingly impossible demands that are made on her. The partner's support of the mother is often a vital factor in protecting the baby from the periods when the mother is depressed or angry, and in helping retain a sense of perspective. Single mothers can gather this support from their parents and extended family as well as from friends.

The baby's innate disposition at birth (additionally affected by the birth experience itself) ensures that all babies arrive in the world outside the womb as little characters in the making. Some babies arrive with placid, self-contained and tolerant natures; others can be little powerhouses of intense, raw feelings. Clearly the baby that possesses a capacity to tolerate a fair degree of frustration will be much easier to care for than the baby who has, in the classical Freudian sense, a larger quantity of id impulses to contend with, and minimal capacity for self-comforting (Brazelton 1984).

Another important factor in the way that mothers and babies start their relationship is the mother's ability to enlarge her capacity to contain anxiety, particularly during the early months of her baby's life. She (or the primary caregiver) needs to be able to receive and process the powerful stream of non-verbal communications of primitive anxieties, as well as positive feelings, that the baby directs at her. This can be pretty over-whelming, with mothers trying to cope with great surges of intense love for their babies as well as intense frustration and dismay when everything feels too much for them. This happens at a time when the mother's hormones are all over the place. Particularly when breastfeeding, there is an emotional lability, which rarely occurs at other stages in the life cycle. In practical everyday terms, this amounts to getting to know the baby and allowing for the unfolding of his or her true self. Getting it wrong and not knowing how to satisfy the baby when it is crying is an intensely anxiety-provoking situation for the mother in particular – and also potentially highly perse-cutory for her (Raphael-Leff 2002).

The kind of baby I am thinking about was described as follows in a parent-infant observation. The observer of the 6-day-old baby girl described her as waking up suddenly, with no quiet stirring period between sleep and wakefulness at all. One moment she was deeply asleep, the next she was roaring and full of desperate hunger. The observer described how she dived into the breast and gave out long sucking and snuffling sounds. Her legs moved in a slow piston motion as if in ecstasy. The observer noted that 'It was as if the milk was reaching right down to her toes.' This vigorous baby arrived with technicolour needs which, although they made her easy to understand, could not always be satisfied however hard the mother tried. In this instance she was the second child of a tolerant mother in a stable relationship. When her baby's demands were exhausting, she would often say, 'Just as well she wasn't my first – I wouldn't have had any more.' One can well imagine how such a child, born to a less mature mother, as the first-born, could be experienced as highly persecutory. If the mother already has a poor self-image and mental health problems, her difficulty in comforting her child in distress is likely to reinforce her perceptions of herself as 'bad'. Some mothers may become depressed at this point – others become angry.

From my experience of the way in which John 'dived' into therapy, and the immediate powerful nature of his projections, I suspect that he may well have projected his feelings with unusually intense power from birth. His mother had an explosive temperament which, she was well aware, was not readily able to contend with the extra strains that motherhood put on it. John was also her first-born. The net effect of this until well on in John's therapy was, to quote his mother: 'When he's mad, I'm mad; when he's in a good mood, I'm in a good mood.' Rather than receiving and processing her child's hostile feelings, she furiously flung them back at him, frequently with her own fury added to them. Similarly, when they both felt happy, they amplified each other's moods into something that felt wonderful. These two states of mind had to be kept entirely separate within John and his mother's relationship.

The shattering experience of going from 'good' to 'bad' was to become increasingly familiar in John's therapy, until we finally landed in a period of therapy which was purely 'bad'. During the many months that we struggled through this, if I had not had my memories of the phase of intense positive transference and counter-transference I, just like John's mother, could have easily come to believe that it was all a figment of my imagination and had never happened in reality. By remembering all of the relationship, and knowing John in the round, and not only in the one-sided way that had developed between him and his mother, I was able to bring the two sides of this split relationship together in my mind. The period of mutual adoration greatly contributed to my being able to do this.

Persecutory eyes and loving gazes

The theme of intimacy which was shattered was well established in therapy, when sad external circumstances intervened, adding further pressure to the central problem of how to contain painful, angry and loving feelings in the same mind and heart. John's father died, unexpectedly for John, despite his long illness. Initially John's efforts at coping with his grief were impressive, but after a few weeks all signs of more ordinary mourning disappeared. He plunged into a hopeless, disintegrated state, in which many of the previous indications of his emotional recovery disappeared. He behaved crazily and self-destructively, indicating that he felt he had nothing to live for. As well as a clearly expressed wish to join his father in heaven, he was busy hacking away at any potential goodness that remained within him. This was very reminiscent of Derek's behaviour (see Chapter 2) when he was lost in his depression. It was a craziness born of grief but quickly compounded by John's sadism towards himself and others. I was very aware of the distress that lay behind his behaviour but unable to talk with him about it as he found this unbearable. He felt unable to share his desperately painful feelings with anyone, and instead became engaged in wholesale destruction around the unit, in the schoolroom, in therapy – in fact, everywhere but on his visits to his home.

His mother, by now a much more integrated and insightful woman than in the past, coped remarkably well with her ambivalent feelings about her husband's death. Significantly, when John felt scared about the bizarre state of mind that he knew he was in, and was frightened that he would be too much for his mother on his visits home (a situation which had prompted physical abuse of him in the past), she was able to understand his fear and reassure him that she wanted to help him with his feelings. She let him know both directly and through the school social worker that he need not be scared to come home to her, and indeed they were able to share their complicated grieving during these weekends together.

Meanwhile John was hurling his craziness into his sessions with me. I was often unable to say anything, let alone interpret any of this process, as it seemed to inflame him further. There was no room for shared insight and as with Derek, I came to the conclusion that I just had to survive. As time went on, the sadism in John's relationship with me worsened. When he found that I did not retaliate to his attacks but struggled to survive and understand them, he took this as a sign of weakness and sadistically redoubled his efforts to frighten and hurt me.

Several months after his father's death, a new theme entered into the sessions. John started to experience my eyes, and my looking at him, as highly persecutory, particularly at the beginning of the sessions. He would often enter the room violently, banging and kicking the door and furniture, shouting that he did not want to come. He would shout at me, 'Don't look at me!' and I would have to avert my gaze until I gradually felt, later in the session, that it was not so persecutory for him. Not being allowed to look at him was at times very painful for me as I was still in touch with my positive counter-transference feelings towards him and very aware of what a distressed state he was in. His mother had had some intermittent mental health problems that had included states of paranoid anxiety. In the transference I now felt that I was with someone who was paranoid and deluded. This was a form of projective identification in which I felt what John had felt in the past, and still felt in the present. It was different to the form of projective identification I experienced when I found myself metaphorically gazing at him with the eyes of a besotted mother, in which I took on the feelings of John's mother in his fantasy.

This feeling of being with someone who was paranoid was particularly acute after the summer break. I was aware that I was really looking forward to seeing John again, but as soon as the session started he commanded that I close my eyes and not look at him, which I felt I had to briefly do. Fortunately he allowed me to talk to him about what this might mean. He seemed to want me to experience what it was like to try to trust someone whom I knew at times could be potentially dangerous to me. I had to trust that he would not take advantage of my closed eyes to attack me. It was a very uncomfortable few minutes for me. I suspected that he had often been in this frightened state of mind when his mother was in one of her odd mental states. I had to recognise how imperative his command was in terms of his paranoid anxiety about my persecutory eyes and how extremely vulnerable he felt to my gaze on his return from the summer holidays.

I was also uncannily aware of the fact that he wanted to study my face as if to try and decipher what mood I was in. I acknowledged how difficult it really was to return to therapy, as he experienced me as someone who stirred up such violent anger and fear within him. He responded, 'Yes – why did you have to come back to see me? Your work is to upset and frighten children, not to help them.' This gave me the opportunity to say to him that he seemed to have two different Monica's in his mind: a Monica who cared about him and whom he liked and had missed, and a Monica whom he felt hated him and whom he hated in turn. He asked me seriously, 'Does that mean there are lots of Johns as well?' These were the first signs that the different aspects of John and myself could potentially coexist within John's mind.

However, the further integration that was now starting initially increased John's anxiety and sadism alarmingly, as the split images that he had always maintained started to come together within him. This process finally came to a head when, after a number of frightening and violent sessions, I found myself questioning the wisdom of continuing his therapy in its present form. I toyed with ideas of reducing the number of sessions or setting a termination date. In view of everything I felt for John in the therapeutic relationship, this was an extraordinary point to have reached. I felt physically frightened of him by now, and think I was at risk at times of him deliberately injuring me. There was also a considerable risk of him hurting himself. He had some control over this increased level of violence to himself or me but this was wearing very thin at times. I made sure that a member of the unit staff was able to hover close by to the therapy room during his sessions, in case we needed help. John knew that I had made this arrangement.

Fortunately I recognised my thoughts about setting a termination date for therapy as a veiled threat in my mind to reject and deprive John of the therapy that he nevertheless was so deeply involved in. This was a reflection of my fear, despair and anger at what was happening between us. I think that I fantasised that if I cut down John's sessions, or threatened to stop them completely, I would bring him to his senses so that he would actively use what little control he had. If I had acted on this fantasy I would have repeated the pattern of behaviour that had existed between John and his mother. While there was a real need to help him to contain and control his violence, repeating within my mind the traumatic rejections of the past was clearly not the way. This wish, on my part, to retaliate was a counter-transference response that was a long way away from my present relationship wish to help John through this period in his life. While there might have been good reason to make the sessions shorter, or less frequent, as a means of supporting John in controlling his aggressive feelings, if the motivation behind this action was one of revenge or retaliation, this would not help.

Ogden (1979) makes the point that the psychotherapist has to be prepared not only to receive and process the patient's projections but also to allow themselves fully to experience the shared fantasy, understanding its importance for the infant or patient. My fantasy about somehow teaching John a lesson by threatening to curtail our sessions, while at first couched in seemingly rational terms because it felt so unsafe in the therapy room, was nevertheless a form of acting out. I may have needed to genuinely have these sadistic thoughts within me, and think the unthinkable, before John could really feel that his deepest conflict had got through to me. This echoes Carpy's (1989) thinking on the partial acting out of the therapist in the counter-transference needing to be tolerated during some phases of the therapeutic relationship.

Winnicott (1947) argues that the infant needs to hate in order to become real, and that it is only through his or her ultimately unsuccessful attempts to destroy his or her world and primary caregiver that he or she can believe in the reality of that world or person, and thus his or her own self. The commitment within the present relationship that I felt towards John helped me to keep going with the work, but on its own it would not have been enough. The understanding that I gained from working within the counter-transference strand of the therapeutic relationship was essential in order to process and understand the loving and hating feelings and fantasies projected into and aroused within me. These are two different forms of projective identification. I had to be prepared to be both the loving gazing eyes and the hating persecutory eyes for him before I finally had the core conflict located within me.

The therapist 'at risk'

As can so often be the case when the therapist has had thoughts like this about the patient, it was as if John knew what had gone on in my mind during the session in which I wondered about curtailing his therapy. Carpy (1989: 293) describes this experience, clearly stating that 'the analyst's tolerating the counter-transference involves his making links in *his* mind, and it is this which allows the patient to do likewise'. It was a form of unconscious to unconscious communication such as sometimes happens in therapy, and in everyday life. In the next session John started to struggle more successfully to control his physical violence, and was thankfully able to convey his continued hatred of me in the form of symbolic play. However, there was still more to come.

After a few more controlled sessions in which I was able to talk to John about his hatred of me, he entered the session seriously wanting to punch me in the face for something he accused me of having said about him. This had the force of a delusion and indeed in his threats he actually did touch, but not hurt, my chin. This briefly shocked both of us. He grabbed the scissors which I had only recently restored to his box and I realised that he wanted to stab me – but, thankfully, he stabbed the chest of drawers instead. I warned him that we would have to stop the session, but to no avail. When I tried to open the door of the room to get help from the colleague who was hovering not far from the therapy room as arranged, John moved towards the electric socket with the clear intention of inserting the scissors (an old threat of his). I managed to stop him but he then proceeded to attack other items of furniture with the scissors. I did not feel that I could struggle like this with him any further. Because I felt that John was more determined to frighten me than to do himself some real harm, I opened the door and called for help. John knew my colleague well and respected him. My colleague and I restated the obvious fact that John must not endanger himself or me during the session; if he did, the session would have to be stopped. However, we would meet again as usual for the next session. The session was then stopped but John helped to clear up some of the debris before he left.

As a result of John's behaviour, I had come to know what it really felt like to be at the mercy of someone who crazily and deludedly attacked me without my ostensibly having done anything to deserve it. This must have been what it felt like to John when he was on the receiving end of his mother's, at times, paranoid behaviour. I was painfully bewildered by this, despite my understanding of the counter-transference. I had been put into direct contact with the awfulness of this abused child's experience of loving someone who also puts you in real danger. Just as John had needed to be on the 'at risk' register so that the violence in his relationship with his mum was monitored, I was now symbolically also on the 'at risk' register, with the unit staff keeping a watchful eye on us during sessions.

John came to his next session with a mixture of bravado and trepidation. He drowned all my attempts at talking about what had happened in the previous session with mockery and a parody of tears and boo-hooing – which nevertheless brought the possibility of real tears and sadness more readily into the session. A violently painful eruption of feelings started to tumble out of him in the next session.

John entered the room and in a crazy maniacal way, went straight to the electric socket and tried to push some paper clips, which he had specially brought with him, into it. I was horrified and tried to stop him, almost shouting at him in my anxiety about his continued need to test out if it really mattered to me that he didn't hurt himself. Looking back on this response of mine, I think that at that point in time John got a glimpse of me as I really was in the present relationship – someone who was trying to help him, who cared about him, and who was also scared about what was happening between us. Within the present relationship, he saw what Stern *et al.* (1998) would call my 'personal signature', in which he and I were briefly aware of each other's humanity in a very authentic way. Having stopped him, and with hindsight having possibly experienced a very disturbing moment-of-meeting type of experience, I managed to find the words to talk to him about what he seemed to be doing. These words came out in stages in the form of a transference interpretation. The moment-of-meeting in the present relationship preceded it and possibly helped John to listen to what I had to say. I said that I thought that he seemed to be trying to work out how we could connect. Was it only in a shocking kind of way – like getting an electric shock from the socket and being electrocuted – or could it ever become a helpful connection – like an electric plug safely and usefully plugged into the socket? There was much more that might have been understood from his behaviour but these words seemed to be enough for him to stop these dangerous threats of electrocution. He did not act out again in this way in the therapy.

John was now gradually able to let a helpful form of energy flow between us. Prior to this, although he had shown some improvement, he had been unable to introject the projections he had put into me due to his paranoia about me, and my persecuting eyes. He was now steadily able to show genuine signs of attachment to, and dependency on, me. He struggled to control his short temper as he didn't want to hurt me, or waste his session. He protested when it was time to leave and could accept my interpretations about his dependency on me, and his possessiveness of me. He also became able to recognise that there were aspects of his true self that, very much to his surprise, he liked. This was a genuine discovery to him – something he had never been aware of before. He became able to take pride in his abilities to draw, act and sing, and actually carried this further by expressing the wish to take up modern dance, which he discovered he had some talent in. Within the schoolroom he became more able to value his ability to think, and his intelligence.

While these difficult times were going on in his therapy, John's relationship with his mother had grown closer. It remained stormy at times, but the process of mourning the life that could have been with her husband had given John's mother new insight into her need to protect her son from her angry attacks. A strongly reparative process was set in motion within her so that she could now say, 'It's better than it was. We're not angry with each other at the same time any more. I calm him down and he calms me down.' Along with this came a sometimes dizzying feeling of hope and excitement for John's future, which I was, as usual, powerfully aware of, and which we both knew had to be carefully grounded in reality and the continued struggle to overcome the many difficulties which remained in his life.

Different forms of projective identification and their function within the transference relationship

The process of projective identification within the transference strand of the total therapeutic relationship played a very significant part in John's therapy. Ogden (1979) has been particularly helpful in fleshing out this complex process. He delineates three coexisting phases in the process of projective identification. First, there is the *fantasy* of ridding oneself of unwanted parts and getting another person to carry them and 'know what it feels like'. While this can be very controlling of the other person, it does not have to be a negative or destructive process, though it can often be a desperate process (Money-Kyrle 1977). Second, there is an *induction* of feelings in the recipient which are the result of the projective fantasy. For example, when the therapy was in the positive transference relationship phase, I found myself behaving as John's mother had behaved, in a manner that felt imperative and not directed from within myself. It felt as if these feelings did not belong to me, but had lodged themselves inside me. Third, Ogden describes how the projection is processed or digested by the recipient, so that it can then be passed back to the projector in a way that is more understandable and tolerable.

This complete process of projective identification served several import-ant functions that could be seen clearly in John's therapy. It functioned as a primitive defence that sustained a split in John's way of seeing and relating to the world and himself by keeping loving and hating feelings apart; it was a form of non-verbal communication with me and, most significantly for John, it became a pathway for change. This particular form of projective identification could be understood as follows: given that the transference is the re-experiencing in the present of past significant relationships, as projected into the therapist, counter-transference can at times be viewed as the 'parent's' side of the story.

In the total therapeutic relationship with John, I was being compelled by the power of his projective fantasies to split my experience of him and relive the central neurotic conflict of love and hate which had existed with his mother. This had the quality of a reconstruction of his early history and current relationship with her, in which he communicated without words what had happened and continued to happen between them. I played the part of the mother in this drama. When I did not repeat his mother's reinforcement of his split view of their relationship, wonderful or perse-cuting, but insisted on struggling to hold both of these qualities of the relationship simultaneously in my mind, I became the integrative 'other' that John needed to help him process these conflicting feelings. By the end of John's therapy I felt that I knew a good deal about how hard it had been for his mum to try to help him grow up. I knew that hers was also a very painful story to tell, as she struggled with mental health problems, a volatile baby, an ill husband and precious little support until John was placed in the therapeutic unit.

By my emphasis on John's relationship with his mother, I do not wish to give the impression that I underestimate the contribution that John's father made to his development. Although not included in this chapter it was very evident that he had been a containing and calming presence in the family, from whom John had gained a great deal of his creativity, together with his 'capacity to be alone' – in this case, in the presence of his father. Unfortunately, this relationship got swept away whenever John's mother lost control. It was his father who in many ways had helped John in the past to find his true self, but this too had to be kept hidden from his mother, for fear of attack. The material about the hidden treasure and cave relates to this hidden side of John's personality as well as to his positive relationship with his father. As John started to recognise his good qualities and take a pride in them, I had the distinct feeling that he had a fantasy of his father, in heaven as he believed it, being able to see the gifts that were emerging. He took pride in this because he knew his father would have enjoyed these aspects of his true self as it started to blossom.

When John left the unit, which was purely for primary-school aged children, he was much more integrated and able to return to living with his mother and with support attend the local secondary school. He was beginning to see his mother in a more balanced way, as someone who felt guilty about the past and wished to improve their relationship in the present. The unit kept in touch with John and his mother throughout his first year at secondary school, by which time John was able to come off the 'at risk' register. By this point John and his mother could see each other much more realistically. They were both still struggling a good deal with their lives, but they were also very conscious of their wish to live together as best they could. This was far from easy, but at least now it was a possibility because it was grounded in greater understanding, acceptance and forgiveness of the serious difficulties of their past relationship, which had enabled them to live together with more tolerance and love in the present.

Chapter 4

Struggling with perversion and chaos in the therapeutic process: the need for the patient to 'know' the therapist[1]

There are many occasions in clinical practice when the problem of what to do (within which I am including verbal 'doing'), as opposed to understanding the question of 'why', raises great uncertainty in the therapist. I suspect that work with children and adolescents is particularly difficult in this respect as often a great deal of the therapeutic process is embodied in the manner in which the basic boundaries of the therapy are established and maintained by the therapist, and then challenged by the patients. Particularly with very young patients, acting out adolescents and very deprived and fearful patients, the therapist's actions and body language are more likely to be listened to than their actual words. It can be argued that the therapeutic environment in which the therapy sessions themselves take place is as important in facilitating change as the other tools in the psychotherapist's clinical bag. This is the third strand in the total therapeutic relationship referred to in Chapter 1. These activities of the therapist in the real external world need to receive similar thought and scrutiny to the total transference relationship and the contents and quality of the psychotherapist's reverie.

The significance of the therapeutic environment in which therapy takes place is particularly evident when children and young people who need more help than they can get while living at home become members of residential therapeutic units and communities. Such units and communities vary a great deal in the philosophy and manner in which they work. A good number of them are based on psychodynamic principles. Some have child and adolescent psychotherapists on the staff and some of these therapists work directly with the children, while others work only with the staff dynamics (Ward *et al.* 2003).

---

1 Much of this chapter was originally published in 1991 as 'Putting theory into practice: working with perversion and chaos in the analytic process', *Journal of Child Psychotherapy*, 17(1): 25–40. The ideas in the original article have been expanded somewhat in the context of this book.

The psychotherapeutic setting

The children who attended the unit I wish to describe had severe emotional difficulties and at least one parent who remained committed to them. The unit endeavoured to provide a sane, tolerant and thoughtful living environment for 25 to 30 children, with good support for the staff. Its philosophy was based on Dockar-Drysdale's model (1990). It did not have an external consultant who worked with the staff group dynamics but there were many opportunities for the staff to discuss their experiences with the children. I saw some of the children for individual therapy, others for a series of consultations, and heard about others in regular meetings with the staff. This model worked reasonably well for this particular unit. Therapeutic units and communities develop their own unique ways of working and their own unique culture, depending on the person in overall charge of the unit, the type of staff that they then attract and the stage of development of the unit. It has often been noted that the personality of the person in charge stamps a powerful character on the way a unit works. As this is very 'hands on' work, this is not surprising.

The children in this particular unit were not children who were, as it was then termed, 'in care'. They mostly came from families where there was an intergenerational pattern of disrupted and problematic relationships. The children had often experienced serious trauma, neglect and rejection and had caused concern to their families, schools and social workers from when they were very young. Many kinds of intervention had been tried before they were referred to the unit.

There was a careful selection process before a child was accepted at the unit. The most significant factor in accepting children was that they came from families who were struggling to break out of a cycle of intergenerational disturbance and had already shown themselves to be capable of some emotional change. All of the parents were expected to work closely with experienced social workers from the unit throughout the placement. The unit stayed in touch with each family for at least a year after the child left. The aim was to return the child to the family and community and the unit had a high success rate. The children lived in the unit and went home every other weekend and during school holidays. Parents were encouraged and helped to visit their children.

There are many implications of offering psychoanalytic therapy in such a setting and these challenged my previous assumptions about the way in which the boundaries for therapy need to be established and maintained. Initially I imagined that the model I was accustomed to using in an outpatient clinic could be fairly neatly adapted to the demands of the unit. I soon discovered that this was not so, for very practical reasons as well as therapeutic, relationship-based reasons. The boundaries between home, school, social life and therapy are entirely different in therapeutic units. For example, at this unit a child only had to cross the playground from the unit's school to get to and from a therapy session, and there was no buffer zone of a journey – with all the positives as well as negatives that this can imply. The therapy room was in the same building as the children's bedrooms and living accommodation. The children knew each other well and knew who was coming to see me when, as well as who had just returned from a session. There was a responsiveness and sensitivity in the staff's understanding that the children might be distressed or disturbed after a therapy session and appropriate measures were taken to receive them at the end of each session. This helped to consolidate the work done in therapy as well as contain the child better in the breaks between sessions. This awareness of when children were going through difficult times in their therapy extended to surprising tolerance and concern on the part of other children in the school towards children who were in therapy.

On the level of relationships, there was a powerful transference relationship to the unit as a whole, into which a very particular transference to the therapist became incorporated (Hartnup 1986). The degree of support that therapy had in the unit had not been achieved without a great deal of effort on the part of all the staff. This involved the working out of boundaries of confidentiality for the children, while maintaining optimum communication of important information between members of staff. The effect of keeping communication between staff very open was that the children had the ongoing experience of a group of adults who were doing their best to provide a containing environment in which they cooperated with each other. In life experience terms, this in itself was a vital part of the therapeutic function of the unit. Many of these children came from families where the marital relationship had broken down and cooperation between the sexes had been lacking. The experience of the staff group behaving like a 'joint marital couple' brought many of the children great relief and increased feelings of security (Byng Hall 1995).

My experiences of working in this setting have greatly affected the way in which I try to think as wisely as possible about how to communicate with the other key adults in my patients' lives, particularly when children are 'looked after' and have many professionals involved with their care, as well as foster parents. In my view, more often than not, in each case there is no obvious right and wrong way to put this into practice. Each patient and each communication with the other adults in the patient's lives, has to be thought about carefully. There is no magic formula that does not end up being unduly rigid and potentially problematic for either the patient or the network. It is more usually a case of choosing a solution to this question which is the least compromising of confidentiality but also the most pragmatic in terms of keeping the system of adults around the child in the best communication possible, in the current circumstances.

As is only to be expected in work of this kind with a group of such severely troubled children, there were also constant and deep anxieties with which the staff group had to wrestle which were the essence of the work itself. I have described and discussed staff group dynamics as well as a way of thinking theoretically about work in therapeutic communities in greater detail elsewhere (Lanyado 1988, 1989a, 1989b, 1993, 2002). Ward *et al.* (2003) offer a good overall contemporary view of the work of therapeutic communities. As work within therapeutic communities is increasingly appreciated, the recent increase in publications about this work is to be welcomed (Ward and McMahon 1998; Maher 1999; Cant 2002; Sprince 2002).

The outcome of working in such a setting was that, partly out of necessity, I had to become more prepared to be flexible and prepared at times to take what I regarded as some therapeutic 'risks'. Needless to say, on some occasions I got my fingers burnt as a result. However, the degree of disturbance of the children seemed to demand this approach, as I often did not know what *else* to do. I had to change my practice. I suspect that this is the way most therapists develop their work according to the needs of their patients. They have to discover what works for each patient and then try to understand how this relates to their existing theoretical and technical framework. Theory may provide further ideas about possible clinical interventions, but frequently it is the translation of this theory into practice that is problematic. Sternberg (2003) has discussed these issues in great detail and undertaken a thorough review of the literature.

The clinical problem: Nicky

When I worked with Nicky, the difficulty of translating theory into practice was more acute than with any of the other children that I treated in the unit. The therapeutic process, having gone reasonably straightforwardly during the first year or so of treatment, gradually degenerated into a state of anarchy and chaos that was previously quite unknown to me, so that eventually I no longer knew what to 'do'. At the end of some sessions I literally felt that I didn't know 'which way was up'. Intriguingly, it was not that Nicky attacked my capacity to think about the process nor, most of the time, that I felt unable to bear the images and feelings that he communicated. What had been aroused in me was a profound sense of having to uphold and defend what I believed to be morally correct and sane, in the face of my patient's insistent presentation of chaos and perversion. The moral overtones of this stance and the need for this morality to be a genuine expression of my personally thought-out moral code made me uneasy as it could so easily have constituted an intrusion of my own agenda into the therapy. As discussed in the previous chapter, I knew that I had to examine my total response to Nicky very carefully.

As far as was known, Nicky had experienced an incestuous relationship with his father from the age of 3 until he was 8. This involved full anal intercourse and fellatio on numerous occasions. It was also likely that he saw his father abusing other family members. There were strong sado-masochistic components to his father's sexuality. His mother gave a good deal of this information on referral. The horrific details became more known in the process of the therapy. Nicky's response to his traumatic experiences with his father had been to behave bizarrely, and once the trauma was in the open, to communicate fairly freely about it. However, he was able to be reasonably appropriate about who he talked to, and did not flood the other children in the unit with what had happened to him. Probably this was because of his continued attachment to his father and his shame about what had happened.

Nicky's father had had a serious drink problem and his mother described lengthy, verbally obscene tirades and physical violence as being frequent occurrences in Nicky's childhood. She ashamedly admitted to having been drawn into his father's extremely disturbed behaviour, particularly when she was faced with his taunts that she was spoiling his 'fun' by trying to stop him. She denied having any knowledge of his incestuous relationship with their son. Nicky's mother had very low self-esteem and rather than, as she feared, risk the loss of her husband if she didn't play her part in the sexually perverse behaviour, she acknowledged that she had debased herself by becoming at times as verbally and physically depraved as her husband. There were long, obscene slanging matches and violent argu-ments in which furniture would fly. These scenes were part of their sado-masochistic sexual relationship. Their sexual excitement escalated in the course of these rows and ended in intercourse. As both parents were often drunk during these times, it was very likely that Nicky had witnessed their intercourse.

Before the incestuous relationship became known, there were many attempts to help the family because of the children's bizarre and disturbed behaviour. The father's incestuous relationship with his children was not uncovered until well into these attempts to help them. It came to light following police allegations that the father had been exposing himself to local schoolchildren.

Nicky was treated many years ago and incestuous relationships were comparatively rarely known of at the time. The father wanted to have treatment and accepted a place in a sexual offenders unit a long way away from the family. He was on probation throughout this time and had very intermittent supervised contact with the children. He was extremely guilt-ridden and at pains to tell his children how wrong he had been to behave as he did. The children lived with their mother who had extended family close by. Despite her many difficulties, she was surprised that she coped better than she could have imagined with this very difficult situation and showed herself to possess great staying power and the ability to provide considerable security for her children.

In the light of this history it is not surprising that Nicky, who was 8 when he started therapy, brought severe anxieties about intimacy into the transference relationship. The way in which he differed from other sexually abused children with whom I had worked was in his use of perversion both as a method of defence against psychic pain and as a pursuit in its own right. It took me a long while to appreciate that I was dealing with a core of perversity in Nicky which, when activated, permeated his whole personality structure, wiping out the sanity he could own at other times. I was initially more inclined to see him as a severely traumatised child who was the victim of perverse parental behaviour. Recent research on sexual abuse and sexually abusive behaviour suggests that having being sexually abused and witnessing marital violence are significant risk factors in adolescent boys becoming sexually abusive themselves. However, the research also suggests that boys who have not been sexually abused, but have been severely rejected and witnessed marital violence may also become abusive in adolescence. Nicky had not been rejected and hopefully this was an important factor in preventing him from becoming sexually abusive in the future – as indeed was the fact that his abuse had come to light and he was receiving treatment (Hodges *et al.* 1994; Lanyado *et al.* 1995; Skuse *et al.* 1997, 1998). However, what gradually emerged in Nicky's therapy was the kind of perversity which Janine Chasseguet-Smirgel describes as a 'perverse core latent within each one of us that is capable of being activated under certain conditions' (1983: 293). Unfortunately, the incestuous relationship had stirred this side of Nicky's nature. This was not apparent during the early stages of his therapy, but in time it became a central feature of our work together.

In this discussion of Nicky's therapy, there are of necessity many important themes and issues that I cannot take up in the context of this book. My focus is on the way in which Nicky's perverted state of mind came to permeate the therapeutic process and how I came to understand this and then struggled with how best to work with it technically.

Breaking the rules

Therapy had been surprisingly well established, three times weekly for about one year with regular attendance and good use of symbolic play and interpretation, when Nicky started to be interested in whether or not I broke rules. He wanted to know if I ever went faster than the speed limit in my car, and drew attention to the fact that when necessary the emergency services were allowed to break certain rules. Firemen, police and ambulances in these circumstances were all allowed to speed, drive on the wrong side of the road, go through red traffic lights and so on. His enquiries were accompanied by playful or coercive attempts to get me to break the rules of therapy, initially by trying to trick me into telling him about other children's sessions. I was able to talk to Nicky about his need to test out whether I really did stick to the basic rules of therapy, because of his experience of his father's breaking the laws of incest. Nicky feared that I might similarly break these fundamental rules, possibly under the guise of this being 'an emergency'.

Until this point in therapy, there had been a growing intimacy between us and the therapeutic process was not any more difficult than with many of the children in the unit. However, the more Nicky was in touch with his strong wish to get closer to me, the more this revived memories, good and traumatic, of his father. This was further complicated by his profound sense of loss of his father in reality. He missed his dad despite everything that had happened, and he often felt very lonely.

A new pattern gradually emerged in Nicky's therapy. It seemed to creep up on us imperceptibly, until it became a big problem – possibly in the way his father's perversity crept up on him. Nicky seemed to have a compulsion to create a perverse situation within the heart of the therapy. At his worst, I would hear Nicky approaching the therapy room, shouting obscenities and on entering the room he would hurl his box of toys at the wall. There was usually no precipitating factor for this behaviour externally, and he rarely behaved in this violent or abusive manner outside the therapy room. When I was forced to stop him from causing damage to the room or myself, with words or action, he would spit at me, attempt to hit or kick me, and become verbally obscene. Sometimes he would deliberately cough up catarrh and spit it on my vacant chair or dangle it tauntingly and revoltingly in front of my face, making me feel quite sick. Frequently there was an orgiastic quality to what he was doing and he would attempt to entice me into his 'game' by being alternately seductively playful, or threateningly violent. He often left the room suddenly when this behaviour threatened to become completely out of hand, only to return shortly afterwards to repeat the whole procedure. He would be grinning and triumphant if I tried to understand and contain his behaviour until I felt that he was making a mockery of my tolerance. His exits and entrances to the room were a safety valve for him as well as a desperate attempt to retain some control over what he felt to be the potentially dangerous intimate relationship with me.

Nicky's behaviour bewildered me and left me full of uncertainties. While I understood it as a communication about the sexually abusive experiences he had suffered, I was very unsure about what I should actually be doing in response, because words, for different reasons to the work with the children discussed in previous chapters, had become useless. I now found myself wondering whether the uselessness of words, which at other times were valued, reflected Nicky's experience of sometimes having a father whom he could talk to, but at other times, particularly when he was being abusive, there being nothing that Nicky could say that made any impact on his father. It was very likely that he had also been completely at a loss over what *he* should do.

In the context of therapy, I now found myself wondering about all sorts of responses to Nicky's violent and abusive behaviour. Should I follow him when he left the room? Should I stop him as soon as he threatened me in any way? At what point should I stop the session, and could I stop it on the grounds of his deliberately disgusting behaviour alone, which felt so personally and terribly abusive? Should I be able to tolerate this better than I did? Would other therapists do a better job with this boy? What was I doing wrong that we had descended into this chaos? Was this a negative therapeutic reaction and could I do anything to redeem the situation? Would a short break in therapy lower the perverse heat of the sessions? Should we be meeting less often? Above all, I felt that what Nicky was expressing was deliberately and personally sadistic and disgusting to me and that I was in danger of perpetuating and appearing to collude with this perverse relationship if I did not find some way to curtail it. I was faced with an anarchic experience which demanded a clear and boundaried response, but I was very confused about what was the wisest course of action.

I was reassured by Meltzer's recommendations in the introduction to *The Psychoanalytic Process* (1967: 13). He advises that in terms of technique 'the secret is simplicity' and that therapists should always work well within the limits of their physical capacity and psychic tolerance. In Meltzer's words, this allows the therapist to 'preside over the setting' and to form an alliance with the most mature part of the patient's personality in the manner which is sought and fostered in psychotherapeutic work.

Prior to this period in therapy, I had had ample evidence that Nicky had often felt disgusted and literally sickened by the sexual relationship with his father, as well as frightened and intimidated. There were also strong loving feelings and painful feelings of loss each time his memories of his father or his relationship with him entered into the therapeutic process. One of Nicky's ways of coping with the absence of his father was to identify with him in his perversion. This was one of the many factors that intensified the grip that perversion had on his whole personality.

Over time, and with much of this time spent in a very disturbing therapeutic reverie, I decided that I had to find a way to say 'no' to Nicky in the way in which he had wanted, but been unable, to say 'no' to his dad. I'm not sure now whether what was needed was a 'no' or the boundary of 'enough'. Nicky and his mum had been unable to stop his father out of a mixture of fear and their own perversity that had been stimulated by his behaviour. But as with many survivors of sexual abuse and violence, what they had most wanted was that the abuse should stop, not necessarily that they lose the aspects of the relationship that they still valued. It was these valued aspects of the relationship that had made it particularly difficult for them to willingly disclose the abuse. Nicky's father had had a very traumatic childhood, and as became evident after the incest was disclosed, genuinely suffered terrible guilt about what he had done. He had actually needed someone to say 'enough' to him before he could accept the treatment for his perverse behaviour that he knew he needed.

Nicky's behaviour disgusted me and was unacceptable. On the basis of our past total therapeutic relationship which had been hard-working and real, I felt confident enough of the resilience of our relationship to feel that it could withstand my saying 'no' (or 'enough') to him. Although I had had my head filled with terribly perverse images I was not drawn into joining in with his sexually perverse 'games'. However, what he had stimulated within me were thoughts about where the boundaries lay within psychoanalytic psychotherapy. I was increasingly unsure where these boundaries lay in his treatment and how far it was appropriate to stretch them in response to the pragmatic demands of the therapeutic situation. I did however know that I really could not tolerate his spitting and catarrh flinging. I didn't need to link it with the sexual games he had witnessed or taken part in, as he was so explicit that his spit and catarrh were semen. I decided that I would start by saying 'no' to this and see where it took us. The next time I saw Nicky, I told him that I could not accept him doing this in the sessions and that if he did I would have to stop the session for the day. I emphasised that I wanted to see him and work with him but was not prepared to put up with his extremely revolting and threatening behaviour, which I knew he was able to control if he chose to. He swore a great deal at this but he managed to stay in the room, and even to share some further very distressing memories of his father's sexuality in what remained of the session.

Nicky needed to know that not only would I not join in with, become excited by, or get vicarious satisfaction from his perverse behaviour and fantasies, but I was also determined to insist that he try to control as much of his behaviour as he possibly could. The insistence that patients use as much self-control as they can muster over feelings and actions that are not sufficiently inhibited is important with patients like Nicky. He was not a neurotic child who had repressed or inhibited sexual or aggressive feelings. He was quite the opposite and seemed to be relieved that I had drawn a line. The behaviour still recurred with less intensity at times in the sessions, but I just reminded him that this was not acceptable, and in the main he stopped it. Certainly the worst of it ceased and Nicky was left in no doubt about what I thought and felt about it.

The *Oxford English Dictionary* (OED) definition of perversion is 'deliberately or stubbornly departing from what is reasonably required, intractable, preference for abnormal sexuality; to turn aside from proper use or nature, to lead astray from right behaviour or beliefs, to corrupt, brutalise, denature, mistreat, degrade, debase'. There are strong moral implications in all these definitions which require a belief in what is 'right', 'proper' or 'natural'. Therapeutic work towards psychic growth assumes a framework of creative order and development based on such beliefs. Although much time is spent analysing destructive forces within and without the individual which are counter to this process, it is unusual to find oneself personally defending these fundamental beliefs in the course of therapy. Aggressive attacks on creativity at the very least implicitly acknowledge that creativity exists. Perversion seeks deliberately to invert and negate such beliefs as well as any existing order and sanity in the universe.

The need of some patients to 'know' the therapist

During this period of therapy there was another intriguing theme taking shape. Nicky became increasingly desperate to know about me as a real person outside what he seemed to recognise as being his fantasies about me. This was partially expressed through his frantic attempts to break into the locked drawers in my room and by increasingly rare periods of symbolic play when he would 'bug' my room, telling me that this was so that he would know what I was doing when I was not with him. While this could have been understood on the Oedipal level, or as a manifestation of his rivalry with other children, this did not seem to be uppermost in his mind. He would also try to take me unawares – for example, by barging into my room when it was clear that I was there but not seeing anyone, by climbing onto the flat roof outside my room to look through the window and by carefully examining my car. He would often be waiting in the staff car park when I arrived at the unit and frequently managed to be in the vicinity when I left. When I asked him about this, he was quite open about the fact that he was spying on me.

This was happening during the period of time when he was in terrible conflict about coming to his sessions, had great difficulty entering my room and was behaving disgustingly. His drive to learn about me had the quality of a quest after truth. He seemed to want (and need?) to know who I really was. Although his emotional fragility meant that he had difficulty staying in class, he had a very searching mind and was capable of excellent project work. This search for knowledge (about me) had a constructive feel about it, and seemed to be a part of the epistemophilic instinct that Klein (1932) describes. Most of the time it did not feel persecuting to me. It felt as if Nicky was trying to check out that whether I had any hidden perverse parts. He needed to know me as a real person, as well as in the therapeutic relationship.

I knew that he hung around my room when I was not in the unit and when he succeeded in finding out anything about me was enormously relieved if he discovered that I did very ordinary things when I was not with him, such as eat my sandwiches at lunchtime or watch television in the evening. I felt that above all he needed to know whether I was essentially ordinary and sane, and whether I had an ordinary sexual relationship with my husband. I could talk to him about this curiosity without telling him anything about myself that he had not already ferreted out for himself.

Thinking about this material afresh, this need to know who I really was also relates to more recent clinical accounts of work with children who are believed to have been ritually abused, or have been victims of a paedophile ring (Sinason 1994; Mollon 1996). This was possibly the case for Nicky in addition to the incestuous relationship with his father. Children such as these often have apparently very ordinary relationships with their abusers in the daytime but at night the abuser is someone entirely different in the way he or she relates to the child – involving disguises, costumes and rituals. This experience is totally denied by the daytime character, so that the child's experience of reality is deeply affected and it becomes very difficult to know what and who is 'real'.

Knowing the 'real' me, was therefore particularly important to Nicky. But, being relatively ordinary and sane is not all it takes to conduct psychotherapeutic treatment. Remaining ordinary and sane in the face of my patient's persistent attempts at perverting the psychoanalytic process was my biggest problem. What he finally raised in me was enormous confusion about what was 'right' and 'wrong', in psychoanalytic terms, in my technique when working with him. Nothing seemed certain any more, as I was constantly confronted with crazy situations that I had somehow to respond to. A state of anarchy kept entering into my thinking about Nicky and how to establish sensible boundaries for his therapy.

If my room had become too persecuting for him, in fantasy and reality, would it help to have another adult whom he trusted close at hand, or maybe in the room for all or part of the session? By chance this had happened briefly on one occasion in the past and had been helpful. I wondered if it would help if I introduced new toys which might facilitate him talking or playing symbolically as he had in the past. When I eventually did try this, the soft toys and teddy bears that Sinason (1988) suggests as helping sexually abused children to express themselves immediately elicited graphic sexual material. Introducing new armies of soldiers, tanks, fighter planes and artillery also helped Nicky to express himself better at times.

However, despite Nicky's great difficulty in coming to sessions, he nevertheless often managed to communicate by action, in an intense brief burst, a feeling or thought that I could work on. I would then, in a similarly brief burst of psychoanalytic activity, feed this back to him through a comment or interpretation when he next managed a few minutes in my presence. For example, Nicky spent a complete session visiting an unwell child whom he hardly knew, but whose room just happened to be close to the therapy room. He chatted to the boy charmingly, joked with the cleaner and a careworker who came into the room, but refused point blank to come into the therapy room. He tried to kick me when I suggested it. Meanwhile, I knew that he was intensely aware of me, as indeed I was intensely aware of him, while I sat on my own with the door open, toys out, waiting. I spent nearly all the session thinking about what he was communicating and wondering how on earth to share my thoughts with him. This was a deeply disturbing form of therapeutic reverie which during this stage in his therapy preoccupied me a great deal during his session times as well as in between his sessions. But however awful this phase of therapy was for me, it was much worse for him.

Shortly before the end of the session I went into the ill child's bedroom and said to Nicky in front of the other child, 'I've been sitting, waiting, feeling left out all this time – which is what I think you wanted me to feel.' He said, 'Good, serves you fucking well right!' He was clearly very pleased with himself and went back to class like a lamb when I told him it was the end of the session. Thinking about the Oedipal issues raised when there is an incestuous relationship, Nicky may well have had very confusing responses to feeling excluded by his parent's sexual relationship. The mixture of relief and rejection is likely to have been very disturbing. I have to confess that there were times when I was relieved when Nicky could not stay in the room for long, as he was so hard to be with, and this was one of those occasions. But I also felt left out and unwanted – which was the part of the experience I decided to share with him.

Our work for the day had been done, but in what a chaotic and crazy way. Boundaries were broken, but thinking and communication had still gone on which seemed to have elucidated some further understanding. But what about the other school pupil, the cleaner, and the careworker who had all been indirectly involved? Would I have been wiser to have done nothing? What do you do with a patient who, to return to the *OED* definition, 'turns aside from the proper use or nature' of therapy, yet nevertheless still seems able, in some extraordinary way, to make use of transference interpretations? Had he succeeded in activating a perversity within me towards psychoanalytic technique which he was now attempting to prove to me was harmless (like his earlier attempts to lure me into his perverted behaviour), or was I breaking the rules in an emergency? He had certainly succeeded in bringing home to me how readily I could get sucked into behaviour which I would previously not have contemplated, and had given me a real insight into the type of seduction that he had been involved in.

At the height of my confusion, I found that my only refuge was in maintaining a sort of sphinx-like position, in which the need to hang onto rational thought and problem solving prevailed. I knew that in the main Nicky could be trusted not to create havoc when he left the therapy room during sessions and that unit staff were on hand to support the therapy. I acted in the belief that the healthier part of him was deeply involved in the therapeutic process and that he would be drawn back to the room out of a driven curiosity about me and what I was doing as I sat there waiting. This intrigued him and indeed did draw him back to the room again and again, despite his fears. My continued efforts to hang onto ordered, rational thinking were often all that remained from the tatters of a therapeutic process. I had to behave with as much dignity and sense of what was the 'right' way to proceed as I could muster.

Theory as an aid to clinical practice

In my efforts to elucidate any psychoanalytic process out of this chaos, I was reminded of Janine Chasseguet-Smirgel's paper 'Perversion and the universal law' which made a great impression on me when I first read it. She talks about perversion as an attempt to take the universal laws of nature and turn them upside down so that chaos prevails and all order and differentiation cease to exist. She says that 'The bedrock of reality is created by the difference between the sexes and the difference between generations' (Chasseguet-Smirgel 1983: 293) and that 'erosion of the double difference between the sexes and the generations is the pervert's objective' (p. 294). She goes on to discuss the biblical laws on incest (Leviticus XVIII) in which the central prohibition is that one should not break the barriers that ensure that the essential laws of nature are preserved. Indeed, *nomos*, the original Greek word for law, means 'that which is divided into parts'. In other words, division and separation are intrinsic to the fundamental concept of natural law.

The fantasy world of Sade is a prime example of perverse thought in which these barriers are demolished. Every permutation of erotogenic zones and their functions takes place in the belief that they are interchangeable. Differences of the sexes, generations and bodily zones are abolished and mixture and chaos are revered. The natural law is turned upside down and the results grossly idealised. Chasseguet-Smirgel (1983: 296) says that the result is that 'the abolition of differences prevents psychic suffering at all levels: feelings of inadequacy, castration, loss, absence and death no longer exist'. Anarchy and chaos are worshipped and morality, in the sense that is intrinsic to any concept of psychic growth, is scornfully ridiculed.

If one stays with the idea that the 'abolition of differences' is a central aim of perversion, it is not surprising that the boundaries which are a normal part of the therapeutic setting should have come under a very particular kind of attack by my perverse patient. I was quite literally no longer sure of where the physical boundary of Nicky's sessions lay. Was it only in the therapy room, or was it permissible to make 'emergency inter-pretations' in another child's bedroom? Did this amount to a perverse breach of technique? While it would be possible to think of this as a type of attack on my containing function this would not have been quite accurate.

When Nicky was at his most perverse he had only a very tenuous and contemptuous belief that such a function existed. It did not feel relevant and alive for him and he simply paid no attention to it. He more genuinely believed in a world where chaos prevailed in an infinitely more potent form. My boundaries were the object of his derision and contempt.

Having gained this theoretical understanding from Chasseguet-Smirgel's paper, I was still left with having to decide what to do in the sessions. I came to the conclusion that my only way forward was to continue to act on my belief that rational thought, natural boundaries and psychic growth *do* exist. I was going to have to rely on the strength of my belief eventually to overcome the power of his belief. All of this seemed to be a far cry from psychoanalysis. It seemed to be more of a morality tale. But I think that dealing with perversion highlights what have to be the therapist's fundamental beliefs in the capacity of life and creativity to transcend the powers of decay and destruction. A strong sense of morality is possibly required in these circumstances to neutralise the opposing tug towards immorality. While in ordinary circumstances there may be some discussion about what is meant by 'morality' and 'immorality', sexual perversity of the kind that Nicky was attracted to is not an area where equivocation is possible. However, this does not mean that the therapist has any room for appearing self-righteous. Additionally, it could be argued that some acceptable levels of therapeutic optimism may be quite ordinarily present in all therapists when they hope that they can help their most seriously disturbed patients toward psychic growth. It is possible to embody this belief while still adhering to Bion's valuable adage that therapists should be 'without memory or desire' in their attitude to their patients (1967).

In terms of process it was possible to discern the following cycle in Nicky's therapy. In his saner moments, often after a holiday or weekend break, Nicky trustingly brought painful material to the session that we could work on together. To my surprise, he seemed to cope with my absence (as he did with his father's) by identifying with me and internalising our relationship. He would then briefly feel more contained, stronger and closer to me. However, these feelings quickly built to such an extent that he felt he could not bear the fear of losing me or having to leave me at the end of the sessions. This intimacy would trigger memories and fantasies which related to his perverse relationship with his father, which were so alive that they were deeply disturbing for both of us. They suggested that Nicky may have experienced sex with strong ritualistic and sadomasochistic components. My counter-transference experience of a battle of beliefs – in which my belief in a sane universe had to be stronger than his belief in anarchy and chaos – reflected what I had only come across in novels in the past: the battle of 'good' against 'evil'.

These terrible memories and fantasies sent Nicky spinning into perverse activity of many kinds due to their continued allure, as well as due to

Nicky's use of perversion as a defence against psychic pain. During these times he looked alarmingly pale and ill, and increasingly miserable. The school staff and even other pupils could sense the distress that he mostly kept within him, and empathise with him. The next step in the cycle would be that he became extremely conflicted about coming to see me as, in the transference relationship, I now represented the person whom precipitated this temptation and fall into perversion, as well as, in the present relationship, being the person whom he knew was trying to oppose it. Anarchy and chaos would take over and I would struggle to carry on thinking and feeling, despite the apparent absurdity (from Nicky's contemptuous point of view) of doing so. Eventually my persistence would pay off and Nicky would struggle to return to his therapy again. Following careful re-establishment of the boundaries, we would try again.

Technically, it is difficult to be sure about what helped Nicky most to keep on trying to live in a non-perverse world. I often avoided interpretations, particularly of a sexual nature, as the precariousness of his psychic balance could not tolerate any further anxiety. He was quite likely to hear any sexually related comments in a highly concrete way, and take this to be a collusion with the perverse side of his personality. If he was at that moment in time managing to function reasonably sanely, I did not want to disturb the balance. This is often an issue with ordinary latency children who are at the best of times attempting to put their infantile sexuality to rest. Alvarez and Wilson both discuss this need to support the appropriate latency defences (Alvarez 1989; Wilson 1989). Hopkins, in her paper on foot and shoe fetishism, also avoids enflaming the passions of her patient in order to create and maintain an area in which they can work (Hopkins 1984). Transference interpretations were helpful when Nicky was in a less disturbed state, but I relied at times on what could have been unworked-through counter-transference experience in order to make them. My ruminations during the times I sat in the room on my own were as much for my sanity as for Nicky's. I had little opportunity to check out my thinking directly with him before launching an emergency interpretation at him. It felt very risky.

The school setting was undoubtedly one of the main reasons we could continue therapy at all. It was often only by discussion with other members of the staff that I was able to see the point in continuing the therapy. The staff felt that although Nicky was so clearly very troubled, the therapy was containing his feelings because he was not acting out in the unit in a way that gave them any serious cause for concern. In addition, the essential sanity and order of the school brought great solace to Nicky outside his sessions.

Sandler argues that 'whatever facilitates the analytic process is therapeutic and whatever moves us away from it is counter-therapeutic' (1988: 4). In effect, if a particular technical or theoretical approach consistently fails to help the therapeutic process forward and therapy is stuck, there may be times when experimenting somewhat with established technique for a particular patient under 'emergency' conditions may be necessary. However, the type of abused and traumatised child that I saw at the unit seemed to take me from one emergency situation to another. These children were so difficult to treat that doubts were often expressed about their suitability for psychoanalytic psychotherapy, owing to their particularly disastrous early experience and their subsequent propensity to action rather than thought and words. Indeed, there is an argument for not working directly with the child at all when placed in a therapeutic community, but only working through the action of the community and the understanding of the dynamics of the group of children and the staff (Sprince 2002). The wisest use of the psychotherapist in therapeutic units and communities depends on the age of the children and the size, character and sophistication of the unit. Having an external consultant for the unit may be essential in helping the staff to understand and process the anxieties and defences that are part and parcel of the emotional life of such units (Menzies Lyth 1988).

If, as is likely, psychotherapists are to continue to try to help these severely damaged children, there is a need to refine and rethink some technical issues which were originally formulated in work with neurotic patients. It is unrealistic to expect severely traumatised and deprived children to understand or accept what to them appear to be arbitrary rules. It may be necessary at times to go down unfamiliar paths with some children before being able to help them find more ordinary (for us) ways of working. It is a question of therapeutic priorities. Child psychotherapists today spend a much greater proportion of their time treating deprived and traumatised patients than in the past. Technique has to adapt accordingly. Just as psychotic children and severely deprived children demand a different therapeutic approach to that of neurotic children, so do severely traumatised children such as Nicky (Tustin 1981; Boston and Szur 1983; Alvarez and Reid 1999).

It may become necessary to accept that some children are untreatable by psychoanalytic psychotherapy. Before reaching that bottom line it is essential to be sure that as flexible a psychoanalytic approach as possible has been taken to the child. This adaptability is necessitated by the reality of these children's disastrous early experience. Necessity is indeed the mother of invention and that includes what goes on in the therapy room.

Part 2

Transition and change

Chapter 5

Transition and change

There is a group of interconnected concepts around the theme of transition and change that I wish to mull over as a way of setting the scene for the chapters that follow. Other key players in these associated ideas are the roles of play and creativity in the process of change, together with thoughts about the part that living with paradoxical experience plays in this process. All of these ideas spring from the clinical experiences described in the following chapters.

The starting point of my thinking is the question of whether it is possible through therapy to help patients to have a greater sense of continuity of being in their lives – that is, to feel internally more joined up, despite many internal and external disruptions and traumas. Is it possible to change the sense of life being full of uncontrollable and traumatic events that cannot be digested, a life which feels chopped up into traumatic fragments, into a personal narrative that, despite the irreversibility of these events, can begin to make some sense and have a feeling of continuity? The end product will hopefully be a person who has become more able to integrate these experiences into his or her life. The ideas in this chapter, and the clinical examples and discussions in the next three chapters, suggest that one of the processes which can aid this greater integration is an awareness of the potential of working with transitional experiences.

Clinical observation, detailed in the next few chapters, suggests that enabling the patient to dare to play with ideas, and to live with paradox during these potentially mind-blowing times, could help what might be felt to be a massive discontinuity in life to feel more like a transition. This makes me think about how more ordinary transitions in life are negotiated. Ordinary growing up is full of these transitions – going to nursery, starting primary school, moving on to secondary school, leaving school, getting a job, leaving home and so on. All of these external changes will be greatly enhanced, or made more difficult, depending on the internal capacity to approach change in a positive rather than a fearful way. The idea of movement is implicit to these thoughts about transition and change. People who can't change are stuck internally and externally, repeating patterns of behaviour and thought, effectively living in an increasingly stagnant internal world. This was the situation that Hilary in Chapter 7 was so dangerously caught in that she believed the only way out of it was to kill herself.

Thoughts about feeling stuck take me to ideas about creativity and how hard it can be for some people to 'have an idea'. An 8-year-old girl, Amy, who ostensibly came to therapy because of relationship problems, found it impossible to play with the elaborate farm scenes that she spent most of her sessions setting out. She seemed pervaded by a sense of inner emptiness that she could not put any meaning into and seemed deeply frustrated and bored with what she was doing, but unable to do anything about it. She was a child who couldn't play. Amy helped me to appreciate what I knew very well theoretically – that not being able to play is a distressing place to be, whatever the deeper anxieties that lie behind this inability. You can't 'make' a child play, however much she may wish to, and this was the problem that confronted us most in the sessions. I gradually realised how much Amy wanted to play, and indeed knew that outside therapy she looked on enviously at those she saw playing freely. I searched for opportunities to interpret the blocks in her ability to play. Eventually, watching how fearful she felt about even putting a few pieces of railway track together, I simply said that I thought she was very worried each time she started to play, that she would not 'have an idea' to play with. She seemed to find it a mystery where other people got their ideas from – and indeed kept trying to buy her way out of this conundrum by constantly demanding new toys from her parents, as if the toys themselves would give her an idea.

It was a relief to Amy when we recognised that her problem when she was with me centred on how hard she found it to play. This helped her to feel less embarrassed about the fact that she didn't seem to be able to do what she saw children all around her doing – that is, to play in a free and easy manner. This in turn gradually helped her to feel less anxious when she approached the possibility of play. Winnicott talks of the need for the therapist to help a child to play if he or she is unable to do so, but in his typical enigmatic way he doesn't say *how* to do this, although I have found many of his ideas helpful in thinking about this question (Winnicott 1971: 44). I think this 'how' lies in what I now think of as the gradual creation of a 'transitional space' within the therapeutic experience, which can then become internalised by the patient (Lanyado 1991b).

Transitional space

The idea of transitional space and transitional experience is difficult to conceptualise, but once having observed, recognised and experienced it, it is a very fruitful and useful idea to have in any therapeutic bag of tools. As with the other theoretical ideas and technical issues raised in this book, to some readers it will be unfamiliar, unorthodox or even controversial. To others it may not. Such ideas may feel unusual to those unfamiliar with Winnicottian thinking because they are so rooted in theories about growth and development, as discussed in Chapter 1, rather than conflict and anxiety.

However, as I do not believe that there is a 'one size fits all' theoretical or clinical perspective, this is simply another way of thinking about the work that may be helpful in some clinical situations. Indeed, Sternberg (2003) draws attention to the many differing views about the use of transference, counter-transference and interpretation that come from work with adult patients and concludes that 'we should note the need to hold onto a number of thoughts or ideas simultaneously as an important therapeutic skill'. Furthermore she cites Hamilton's (1996) study about how theoretical group orientation influenced individual thinkers, in which as well as finding interrelationships between specific theoretical influences and technical practices, she also found considerable individuality of response.

The concept of the creation of a transitional space in therapy has gradually crept up on me and I now realise that I have been using this idea for a good while without trying to formulate it more coherently. The papers that formed the basis of the first three clinical chapters of this book (Chapters 2, 3 and 4) were written before I was as clear as I am now about what I mean. The three chapters that follow this chapter are based on papers in which I was getting clearer about what I meant. And writing this book has found me enlarging and revising what I mean. So this is very much work in progress.

In particular, my work with children in the process of moving from fostering to adoption, officially known as 'children in transition' has had the effect of getting me to return again and again to thoughts about what is meant by transition and paradox. In my clinical practice to date, I do not think any other work has so clearly illustrated how apparently impossible and yet how imperative change can be. This chapter and the next were originally one paper, but as this paper has been given to many different professional groups involved with these children, and from many different perspectives, I have found the ideas around it growing and growing (Lanyado 1997, 1999a, 2000, 2001a, 2002, 2003a). Not only does the predicament of these children deeply affect all those who work with them, but there is much to learn about children and adults in general, who are trying to change in less dire circumstances.

In essence, I see what I conceptualise as transitional space as emerging slowly from the many small and cumulative experiences that the patient has of being alone in the presence of the therapist. It is an experience which can be thought of as a space in between them, which does not belong to one or the other person. This in-between nature of the space is uniquely created and generated between patient and therapist as the therapy progresses, and is what makes it transitional. It has to do with 'two-ness' creating 'one-ness'. It is similar to the idea that you cannot clap with one hand. Building on Winnicottian thinking, the in-betweenness of the clap itself is what makes these experiences 'transitional'. Initially in therapy, these experiences may be momentary. But if the therapist notices them, and is able to let them breathe a bit and 'be' a bit in the session, they gradually appear more often. Over time the therapist is able to observe more fully-formed ideas, and then ideas which are played with, again briefly at first, begin to emerge within the session. Lesley and Derek in Chapter 2 illustrate this process, as do Sammy and Pete in the next chapter. This is the way in which young children developmentally start to play. The ability grows quietly, initially dependent on the presence of the 'other' to keep it going, and growing.

Neuro-scientific research suggests that early right cortex brain development cannot occur in social isolation – it needs interaction with another person to be catalysed into action, although the potential for it coming into being is present within the brain's way of functioning (Pally 2000). We know that children who have been grossly deprived find it very hard to play in an ordinary, creative way. We also know that autistic children cannot play other than in very limited, ritualised ways, which can hardly be called play, and that they also have great difficulty in communicating with and relating to people as living beings (I have written elsewhere about a-symbolic and symbolic play – see Lanyado 1987).

So it is possible to postulate that a child who cannot play nevertheless may have the potential to play, if the relational conditions allow for this. The therapist may be able to provide this kind of relational environment through his or her concentrated attunement to the patient during the session, together with his or her capacity to notice the tiny beginnings of ideas and play, and then nurture and pay further attention to them. The concentrated attunement on the part of the therapist is what creates the ground for the patient to gradually become aware of being alone in the presence of the therapist, and indeed for the therapist to recognise that this is starting to happen.

However, this nurturing is not a forced activity. In some respects it is more related to noticing the process and attempting not to get in the way of it. Going back to my horticultural metaphors at the start of the book, it is like spotting a new bud on a plant that was none too healthy, and trying to water it, fertilise it, spray it to protect it from disease – that is, give it the best possible chance of continuing to grow. The emphasis is on natural recovery rather than emergency care in a hothouse atmosphere.

In therapy, one process that this often relates to is not commenting on the process, but just trying to let it happen. This is not as passive a process as it sounds as it may involve the therapist having to restrain him or herself from commenting on fascinating material because this might interrupt the process itself. It is incredible how sensitive child patients can be to the therapist's ability to concentrate on the child while this process is going on. On one occasion when this kind of play was taking place in Amy's therapy, my thoughts briefly wandered to other things while she played. To my astonishment, Amy abruptly stopped playing. I decided to say that I thought that she had been aware that my thoughts had briefly gone elsewhere and she had felt dropped by me. I may even have said that I was sorry that this had happened. This enabled her to play again in this way when she next came for her session, although we had lost the thread of the transitional space and the play it had facilitated for that session. Not interrupting this sensitive process while it is happening can be a very active process.

The belief and trust within the therapist that these natural processes of recovery and development really can come back online, given the right environmental opportunities, plays a significant part in this process. The therapist's buoyancy and essential hopefulness about the potential for change within the therapeutic process will be evident in his or her way of being with the patient, from many tiny cues that he or she gives out. These cues can be communicated by the therapist and perceived by the patient both consciously and unconsciously. The quality of the therapist almost watching with baited breath, and certainly being as still and quiet as possible so as not to disturb the process, may be palpable at times. During these periods the therapist is also able to stand back and think about what is happening. This is like the stance of a participant observer in which there is a deep receptiveness combined with an ability to remain separate and to think about the experience.

Another way of thinking about the relational aspect of how this process takes place might be by using the image of the way in which two wave forms meet and overlap, forming a new wave form as a result. The patient is represented by one type of wave with a particular wavelength and frequency, the therapist by another. When these waves overlap, while there is a particular contribution from both of the wave forms, there is also a new wave which is created from the individual contributions of the two separate waves. The overlap of two Venn diagrams also illustrates this idea, but in a static form.

The transitional space can also be described as a place in which 'doing' is suspended and the experience of 'being' can potentially emerge. It is a place in which reverie can occur in therapist and patient and it is in the *overlap* of these reveries that something new can emerge as a result of the therapist and patient having shared the unique experience of inhabiting this space (Ogden 1999). Ogden's work, as he acknowledges, owes much to Winnicott's statement that 'Psychotherapy takes place in the *overlap* of two areas of playing, that of the patient and that of the therapist. Psychotherapy has to do with two people playing together' (Winnicott 1971: 44, emphasis added).

There are times when there is a distinctly dreamy, floaty element to this reverie. At other times, those who are interested in meditation have noted that there is a distinct meditative quality to the therapist's state of mind (Coltart 1996; Molino 1997). I would agree that meditative practices that focus on an inner stillness can be very helpful to the therapist in finding a way to be with the patient which has more to do with 'being' than 'doing'. Interestingly, it is also likely that this effort to find stillness and peace is very much in keeping with neuro-scientific work on trauma which focuses on the importance of affect regulation within the therapeutic relationship (Schore 1994). The links between the meditative process and reverie, as well as what can be conceived of as a spiritual or philosophical perspective to the therapist's work, are becoming increasingly recognised and discussed (Molino 1999, Emanuel 2001, Klein 2003). This may be particularly so when there is a stillness and quietness within the room during which the therapist is acutely attentive to the patient and yet simultaneously in touch with what could be thought of as a more 'oceanic' experience.

However, there are patients, particularly those children who are in the care of the local authorities, who for long periods in their therapy are on a different planet to this kind of experience. They are unruly, anarchic, unpredictable, turbulent, aggressive, incoherent and at times very difficult even to keep inside the therapy room – in short, anything *but* still or quiet. How is it possible to talk about these children in the same breath as 'oceanic experience'? Yet which children could need this kind of experience in therapy more than these?

'Tiptoeing' up to children such as these with carefully timed, brief, simple and one sentence interpretations, and watching carefully how well they are able to take these in, is one way of doing this. There is an example of this in the therapy with Derek in Chapter 2. And although this is not reported in the next chapter, a lot of this kind of interpretation had taken place before Sammy and Pete reached the stage in therapy that is described in more detail in Chapter 6. Alvarez has helpfully discussed in detail the importance of what she calls the 'grammar' of interpretations, particularly when working with borderline patients (1997). This extremely cautious, spoon-feeding way of interpreting is also very necessary in terms of the child gradually becoming more able to feel safe enough to expose him or herself to the therapist. It is based on the slow establishment of a growing trust in the therapeutic relationship, in which the therapist is respectful of the child's deep fearfulness of being helpless and out of control – a fear which can be intense when the therapist makes an insightful interpretation which penetrates too sharply into the child's inner world. This can be experienced as an attack, and many children who are 'looked after' will tell their therapist to shut up, or will drown their words of wisdom with noise, or talk over them. If all else fails, the child may cover his or her ears, attack the therapist or rush out of the room.

Adult patients, on recovering from very regressed states, in confidence testify to the importance of the way in which, in the context of a well established treatment, the sensitive therapist largely unconsciously uses his or her body during regressed states and highly vulnerable times for the patient, to facilitate the therapeutic process. For example, this can be evident to the adult patient in the therapist's use of the voice which can be experienced as similar to the sounds a well-attuned mother may make in order to soothe or contain a distressed baby. These patients also testify to the value of the experience of the therapist's stillness, physically and emotionally, at times when the patient is feeling chaotic, overwhelmed and over-reactive. These observations are again strikingly in keeping with the neuro-scientific research discussed in Chapter 2.

The transitional space has certain characteristics that can help the therapist to recognise that the therapeutic journey has reached this place. But, it is still easier to say what this transitional space is not, than to say what it is. Transitional space is the opposite of a space in which the individual feels trapped and unable to breathe, think and play. The sense of being stuck in endlessly repeating negative emotional experiences is a frequent complaint of those seeking psychotherapeutic help. By contrast, a sense of freedom and spontaneity characterises experiences that take place within the transitional space. It is in the transitional space that new ideas and possibilities emerge and can be played with in a safe way. It can be like emerging into an open space after being lost in the woods. But it can be very difficult to reach this place. It is also an in-between place in which past and future are bridged and being 'present' is full of potential (Winnicott 1951). This adds another dimension, that of time, to the idea that this space is 'transitional', in this sense existing in between past and future and being very much of the present moment.

However, lest this description should sound too much like Nirvana, I would like to emphasise that what emerges in the shape of children's play during these times is often painfully and frighteningly appropriate to their internal dilemmas. The transitional space is a place in which these painful issues can be addressed because the *vehicle* through which they can be expressed – be it play in a child, or free association, dreams and creative thought or expressions in a teenager or adult – has become more available for use. For example, Pete in the next chapter finds an extraordinary metaphor through play for expressing his feelings about leaving his foster family and moving to his adoptive family. Sammy was also able to do this and I have described this in detail elsewhere (Lanyado 1997, 1999a).

It is the acceptance of the essence of this space, that it is neither inner nor outer, past or future, the patient's or the therapist's, but paradoxically both, that contributes significantly to the feeling that this is a space in which anything could happen. It is a space full of potential and surprises where paradox, defined in the *Concise Oxford Dictionary* as 'a seemingly absurd or contradictory statement, even if actually well-founded', can be tolerated. The freedom of playing with ideas relies heavily on the suspension of the ordinary rules of reality, and the suspension of 'either/or' thinking. This is not about the conflict of two opposing forces or feelings, but about the acceptance of their coexistence. This leads to the contemplation of what may seem absurd – such as two opposing feelings being true simultaneously. It could be argued that this kind of apparent paradoxical absurdity has led to some of the most startling innovations in the arts and sciences.

It is important to note that within the confines of therapy the experiences that take place within the transitional space are not without boundaries. This would be potentially too frightening an experience and would be unhelpful. The patient is very consciously 'held' in the therapist's mind, but in such a way that it is possible for the patient to experience what it feels like to be 'alone in the presence of someone' (Winnicott 1958). This idea resonates with Ainsworth's concept of the capacity to feel free to explore because of the internalisation of a secure emotional base (Ainsworth 1982; Bowlby 1988). Within this atmosphere, it is possible for many surprising experiences to take place. New ideas can emerge, new light can be thrown on old thoughts and experiences, and the patient (and therapist) can make discoveries about themselves that are at times quite startling. I have not gone into detail in exploring the therapeutic relationship in terms of attachment theory in this book, although I certainly find it helpful to think in these terms because this has been done so effectively elsewhere (Holmes 1998, 2001; Hopkins 2000).

For many very deprived and traumatised children, the creation of a transitional space can prove enormously elusive. The specific difficulty within each treatment of enabling this space to become alive is one of the processes that therapists have to work with as creatively as possible. Part of the difficulty is the fact that this space may initially be sensed to be more like a chasm or terrifying gap than a place in which it is possible to become more alive (Fransman 2002). Maybe this was part of what Derek in Chapter 2 was expressing with his vivid drawing of a man falling off the edge of a cliff, or indeed what Pete expresses with his train track play in Chapter 6. Much time in therapy may be spent in trying to enable a child to dare to let him or herself to be free enough to 'taste' the transitional space for long enough to become attracted and intrigued by it. Part of the therapist's task is to keep the possibility of entering this space as alive as possible within the therapy.

Another important quality of the transitional space is in terms of what Ogden describes as the 'aliveness' of the sessions, which he sees as an indicator of the therapeutic potential of each session (1999). This is a very helpful concept. Working with children who have been severely abused and repeatedly traumatised from the start of life can lead to profound dismay at the enormity of the therapeutic task. Keeping in mind that therapy has the potential to help the child to become 'more fully alive as a human being' helps to keep the therapist's hope alive. Alvarez (1992) expresses this idea in her work with autistic patients.

The most obvious sign that a transitional space has been established in therapy, and more importantly in the patient's mind, is that the patient becomes more playful and creative. The importance for creative living of the capacity to play cannot be overstated. Parents know this intuitively when they take pride and pleasure in the play of their children. Similarly, when parents bring their child for a therapeutic consultation, they will often mention the child's inability to play in any satisfactory way as a significant symptom. One of the very obvious changes that takes place during any therapy is that, as the child gets better, he or she becomes more and more able to play and to concentrate. Play themes which are highly relevant, symbolically expressing the child's deepest anxieties, defences and conflicts, can then emerge with incredible and poetic appropriateness. Even with the most deprived children this can happen, as illustrated by Sammy and Pete in Chapter 6.

In older children, young people and adults, the quality of playfulness takes over from play itself as an indicator of emotional growth. By this I mean the ability to play with ideas and make unexpected connections between them in the free flowing manner which characterises creative play. Ultimately, this kind of playfulness is the essence of freedom of thought and expression, such as is experienced in great cultural and scientific achievements – for example, the creation of art, drama, music and scientific discovery. The oppression of freedom of thought is such an attack on the individual's sense of aliveness that major historical events, and indeed wars, have resulted from political attempts to suppress the freedom of the individual to think, feel and openly express opinions that he or she believes in.

'Looking forward', mourning and the process of change

The final idea that I wish to highlight as being embedded in these thoughts about movement and the process of change is the importance of recognising how impeded mourning can halt psychic change. Part of the problem in many people's difficulties in moving on in their lives, for whatever reason, is the natural reluctance that is present in all of us, to face the pain of letting go of the past. It is very hard to do, and so we avoid it, defend against it, cling to the past in all its familiarity, however awful that familiarity may be. It still feels safer than going into the unknown, which is implied when change is required.

On the brighter side, I think it is very important that therapists keep in touch with the excitement of change for the better. This will hopefully be the patient's experience at times, when he or she sees real positive changes taking place internally and externally during the course of therapy. This is after all what it is all about, and why patients come for therapy. They are in distress and emotional pain, they cannot make sense of their lives, their relationships are in disarray, and so on. When things start to get better in these areas of their lives, or new interests, opportunities and relationships start to come into their lives, there can be a sense of pleasure and excitement which is often well-deserved and struggled for. But this cannot happen unless there is some movement away from the emotional luggage of the past that is weighing the person down.

Learning how to let go of the past can be difficult even if this is only in terms of unlearning old habits that are consciously unwanted. Mourning lost opportunities or relationships that cannot be righted, as well as mourning the life that might have been had trauma not disrupted it, may be essential before a patient can feel the buoyancy of positive change. Sometimes these feelings happen simultaneously, as with children moving from fostering to adoption. There can be periods of critical change, when establishing the wisest balance between looking backwards and looking forwards is very difficult to achieve. If the individual is to move forward in life, this balance needs to naturally tip towards feelings of hopeful anticipation that, despite the awareness of feelings of loss, enable the patient to greet change. If the balance tilts backwards and is still too much in the thrall of loss, particularly where mourning is clearly impeded, no genuine progress can be made.

The place of ideas about the significance of the presence of the therapist in facilitating transition and change is explored in the next three chapters. In differing ways it is suggested that the presence of the therapist plays an important and at times vital role in these processes. This can be evident in a quieter form of facilitating the creation of a transitional space, or in a noisier form of being intensely present during a moment-of-meeting in which the therapist's personal signature is briefly but clearly seen by the patient.

Chapter 6

Psychotherapy with children in transition from fostering to adoption: a question of technique[1]

The clinical work in the first part of this book shows how difficult it is to help children recover from trauma where family circumstances have remained relatively constant. So it is no wonder that when faced with the enormity of the numerous traumas and grave neglect that 'looked after' children have experienced against an unstable external backdrop, recovery can seem like 'mission impossible'. Yet these children are taking up what seems like an ever-increasing proportion of child psychotherapeutic resources (37.5 per cent in one clinic audit – Fleming 2002), and against the odds do seem to be able to make some significant recovery. A great deal of thought and research is currently being undertaken within the child and adolescent psychotherapy profession around the clinical, technical and theoretical problems that these children present (see, for example, *Journal of Child Psychotherapy* 2000; Hindle 2001, Hunter 2001, Ironside 2002).

My particular interest in how best to help these children and those who live with them has centred over the past few years on thoughts about how the therapist might be able to convert a current potentially traumatic change in care into a creative transition in the child's life. This is most evident when there is a change of foster family, or a move from fostering to adoption. There are different points of view about the wisdom of working with children who are in transition as this appears to go against the therapeutic grain of only offering therapy to a child who is emotionally held within a secure home base. However, it soon becomes evident when working with looked after children that each poorly managed change of

---

1 Much of this chapter was originally published in 2000 as 'Fenomeni transizionale e cambiamento psychico: riflessioni sul ruolo del transfert e della relazione "attuale" nel passagio dall affidamento all adozione' [Transitional phenomena and psychic change: the role of transference and the new relationship as seen in the therapy of children moving from fostering to adoption], *Studi Psicoanalitici del Bambino e dell Adolescente*, 8(3). The paper was given at the third conference of the European Federation for Psychoanalytic Psychotherapy in the Public Sector (EFPP), Rome, Italy, October 1999.

placement just adds to the accumulation of despair and mistrust that the child carries with him or her.

In my work with children who are 'in transition' I have come to realise that quite paradoxically there can be therapeutic potential within these extraordinary circumstances. If therapy can harness this potential, a significant step forward can be achieved in the child's internal world and the new placement has a better chance of surviving the inevitable strains that will be experienced.

Thoughts about attempting to stay with the paradoxical experience that is at the heart of any transition in life link with the capacity to suspend reality for long enough to play with apparently absurd ideas. This idea is central to my thinking. This type of playing is like an emotional chemistry in which two apparently disparate emotional elements combine to form a new emotional compound. It is full of surprises. Psychotherapy that is acutely attuned to the potential for this to happen – almost when it might least be expected, under the strains of placement change – draws on an aspect of the present relationship between the patient and the therapist that actively strives to make the current change very different in emotional quality to the changes of the past.

Most psychic change, within therapy as well as in everyday life, is a part of a continuous process. It does not come out of the blue, but is usually the result of a quiet accumulation of many small and often unremarkable and unnoticed steps, from which some clear benchmarks emerge which indicate that deep change has taken place. I wish to draw attention to the importance of what is going on during the periods in therapy when nothing much seems to be happening, and think about them as transitions between one way of being and another.

These transitions in therapy are not in my experience times of great transference interpretative activity although there may be a good deal of more general interpretative and verbal comment. A helpful transference interpretation might emerge in time, but this is like the tip of the iceberg of all that has gone before. What is it then that has gone before? What is happening in all the time that the transference is *not* being verbalised?

I am going to illustrate and discuss these ideas about transitions in the context of the therapies of Sammy and Pete, both aged 3 when they started therapy. Both children were referred to me with the explicit remit of helping them to move from long-term fostering to adoption. The adoptive homes were in the same area as the foster homes, so they did not have to cope with the additional loss of moving to unfamiliar surroundings, changing school or losing regular contact with social workers who had become important to them. They also did not have to lose their relationships with me as a result of the adoption, and knew that I would stay as emotionally close to them as possible throughout the transition to their new homes. Relatively speaking these were fairly straightforward adoptions.

Both children had suffered serious neglect and deprivation as well as witnessing violence and experiencing physical (and possibly sexual) abuse from birth until they had been taken into care during the first year of life. They were the kind of children I have described elsewhere as suffering from 'multiple traumatic loss' (Lanyado 2001a, 2002, 2003a, 2003b). Children such as these, who can be extremely aggressive and unpredictable in their behaviour, and very hard to care for, are actually showing the results of experiences of trauma and loss repeated many times during their short lives – often from infancy onwards.

Children who are 'looked after' are trying to survive many traumas in the midst of a turbulent and changing sea of separations and losses of attachment figures, together with the availability of potentially new attachment figures, having been severely let down by their primary attachment figures. It is very important to be clinically realistic about how much repair is possible in a lifetime, let alone a few years, after such a start. However, from clinical experience we know that therapy can provide a kind of incubation period during which a new direction can, albeit often with great difficulty, be found in life.

This potential is most keenly felt when a long-term fostering placement or adoptive placement is looked for and the child has to leave a foster home in which he or she has felt safe and accepted, possibly for the first time in his or her life. This was the case for both Sammy and Pete. It was because of the security, care and love that they had received while in their foster homes that they had become 'adoptable'. And yet they had to cope with the intensely paradoxical situation of leaving these nurturing and responsive relationships behind and moving on to unknown adoptive homes where they were very wanted and would have a long-term future.

I am going to focus on the phase of therapy when both children knew that they were soon to meet the adoptive family but had not as yet been told anything about the family that they were to join. They had both been in therapy for at least six months by this time, and therapy was well established. Momentous change was in the air and was probably detected by the children within the foster family environment and in the social worker's attitude – as well as, I suspect, my way of being with them during the therapy sessions. The social workers had been through the process of meeting the approved adoptive parents and telling them about the children, as well as showing them videos of each child in his foster home. The foster parents had also met the adoptive parents. From the start of therapy I attended as many of the review meetings on each child as I could. In addition, I met the adoptive parents to talk with them about the therapy, which they had been encouraged by the social workers to continue for as long as possible after adoption, to ease the transition. There had been complicated planning meetings, in which I was also involved. The purpose of these meetings was to think about and plan how best to introduce the adoptive parents, new family and home to the children, and then how to move through the few weeks when the child gradually got to know the adoptive family and became ready to leave the foster home. I will discuss the technical and theoretical implications of the therapist's involvement with the child's external world later in this chapter.

All of this was going on (supposedly) behind the scenes, and filling the minds and hearts of the adults who were closest to the children, but at the same time the children supposedly did not 'know' exactly what was happening and had to trust the adults as best they could. The many paradoxes involved in this situation felt pretty mind-blowing for *me* to try to think about. What on earth could it have felt like for these already severely traumatised little boys?

This sets the 'therapeutic scene' that I wish to concentrate on. My question at the time was: 'What is the best way that I can help the child, now?' A possible answer came from the children themselves, as I hope to illustrate and then discuss.

Sammy

Sammy had responded to the deprivations and abuse in his past by becoming a real handful for his foster parents, and in his sessions. He was an unruly and at times deliberately naughty and confrontational little boy – but he was also very able to express what he felt and had an emotional and rather passionate nature. As well as driving his foster mother to desperation at times, he could really pull on her heartstrings and was a very appealing and attractive child. She knew that she would find it very hard to part with him, as would her husband.

During the period of therapy that I am focusing on, when Sammy knew that he might meet his adoptive parents soon but had no exact idea when, Sammy started to want to take little bits of paper that he had cut out of drawings he had done in the session home with him. This was a surprisingly creative compromise solution that he suggested, as he knew and understood why I felt that his drawings belonged in the therapy room. I felt that in view of the impending separation from his foster parents that he was so upset and confused about, taking a little 'keepsake' (as it felt at the time) home with him from therapy was probably helpful to him. It felt like a spontaneous solution that he had found to help him cope with what had become a painful separation from me, which was a new feeling for him. Taking the bits of paper was an idea that had not occurred to him before because he had not previously found the end of sessions distressing.

As we got closer to the time of introduction to his adoptive parents, I gradually recognised that these bits of paper could be thought of as being transitional objects (Winnicott 1951) which Sammy was spontaneously creating within therapy and which helped him to deal with the paradoxes, separations and massive changes he was living through. These anxieties were very alive each time he said goodbye to me. This was evidence of his healthier attachment to me within the present relationship strand of the therapeutic relationship (Hopkins 2000), as his previous separation experiences had been much more ambivalent. This transferred ambivalence from his past relationships had been a regular feature of the early part of his therapy, which was why his wish to take a keepsake had such a different and new quality about it.

I observed this development with interest but was still surprised when at the end of a particularly painful session Sammy became desperate to take a green ball from his box of toys (which he had barely noticed before) home with him. This was initially very much against my better judgement, but there was such an urgency expressed in his wish to take the ball that I let him do this, as long as he bought it back to the next session – which he agreed to do with his foster mother's support. It was the imperative nature of his wish to take the ball that persuaded me to let him take it, and this was after only a brief disagreement.

After the session I realised that I was giving his acquisition of the ball my blessing, rather than letting it become to him like a theft or a triumph over me. Because of the earlier wish to take bits of paper home with him, I was by now alert to the similarity between the way in which he had 'created' this object (the ball) for himself and claimed rights over it, and the way that a baby will *discover* his or her own special blanket or soft toy, that becomes the classical transitional object as described by Winnicott (1951). This was an important sign of emotional health and development in the midst of an otherwise internally and externally tumultuous period in his life. It was the kind of sign of emotional health that I feel it is so important to recognise in its earliest stages, and encourage. It was a surprising achievement for Sammy, particularly considering the turmoil he was in. My acknowledgement of the importance of the ball to him in turn may have helped the ball to become all the more significant for us. However, immediately after the session I was convinced I had made a mistake in allowing this, and would now have to battle with him as he gradually removed more and more toys from his therapy box to his home. This did not in fact happen.

Throughout the weeks that followed, during which time Sammy was introduced to his adoptive family and left his foster family, the ball came and went, to and from the sessions with Sammy. It was played with and carefully looked after as well as at times aggressively knocked about, both in the therapy session and at his foster home. His foster mother intuitively understood that the ball was important to him. Even when he forgot to bring it to the session he always referred to it. It was very clearly neither his nor mine – and this was a paradox that I deliberately maintained as it belonged to the nature of the paradoxical but potentially creative experiences Sammy was going through.

After a rocky start, Sammy settled well in his adoption. And what happened to the green ball? It went with Sammy to his adoptive home, made a few more visits with him to his therapy sessions and then, as he settled into his adoptive home, it gradually lost its meaning to him. I would like to think that rather like his relationship to me after the end of his therapy, it was not so much forgotten as relegated to limbo (Winnicott 1951). In this respect, therapy itself can be seen as a transitional experience, with the therapist functioning as a transitional object, helping the patient to make the move from one way of being at the start of therapy, to another at the end (Lanyado 1999a). Hurry and her colleagues discuss and illustrate a similar idea, in which they persuasively argue that the therapist is a developmental object for the patient, as well as a transference object (Hurry 1998).

Sammy's therapy took place before Pete's and alerted me to the possibility of transitions having the potential to become creative, as well as the potential for new transitional phenomena to emerge during this time. This helped me in my understanding and response to Pete.

Pete

Pete had gained a great sense of stability and security from his two years of being with his foster family. For a long while, he had coped with his misfortunes by withdrawing into himself. During the therapy that preceded his readiness for adoption, he had changed from a toughened, withdrawn, traumatised and unnaturally muscular child, into a sweet, cuddly but very confused little boy. He had a lot of developmental ground to make up.

Perhaps because of Sammy's treatment I had become more alert to the kind of play I shall describe. I knew that the adoptive family had decided that they wanted to adopt Pete and that the whole process of 'linking' was starting. Pete did not know this, and because he lived in a rather self-protective haze a lot of the time, he had expressed few intense feelings about the loss of his birth mother and no longing for a new mummy and daddy. His foster mother said that he did not seem to understand what adoption meant, even though he would have heard the word quite often within the foster home that he shared with another child who had been adopted while Pete was there. He didn't seem to feel that he had ever had a mummy and daddy, neither did he feel that he would ever have them in the future. He had been coming for twice-weekly therapy for seven months when the session I shall describe took place. The concept of being adopted seemed to mean very little to him despite his foster mother's attempts to talk to him about his social worker hoping to find him a family he would live with 'for ever'.

In his therapy until this time, Pete had had great difficulty staying with any theme in his play for more than a few minutes and generally seemed to haphazardly play briefly with one toy and then another. For much of the time, his play did not seem to satisfy him or express anything meaningful for him. He had not paid much attention to the wooden trains and track (which were shared toys) before, but in this session he started to play with these in quite an imaginative way that was unusual for him. He connected two trains together and placed them on a single piece of track, running the trains to the end of the track and stopping them there. He then added another piece of track, and carefully moved the trains to the end of this piece, and so on until he had built a section of track with a number of pieces in it. He was unusually quiet and intent on this play, as if he was trying to work something important out, and I felt I was interrupting him when it was the end of the session.

At the time I wondered whether the way in which he built up his track would be a useful way of talking to him about not knowing where the Pete-train was going and how he was literally finding out as he went along the track. Two sessions later he arrived and said, 'Jane [his social worker] is getting me a mum and dad!' He was delighted, excited and rather astonished by this news.

At the following session he went straight to the train track and spent the whole session playing with it. He had never managed this level of concentration before. He made up the track in the same manner as before, piece by piece, moving the train to the end of each piece as he built up the larger train track. He had an idea that when the train came to the end of the track, it risked 'falling into the water' – which was why more track had to be added. He was particularly fascinated with a piece of track that forked into two directions, and spent a lot of time manoeuvring the train backwards and forwards along the two alternative routes of this junction.

I watched this play quietly for about 30 minutes. It was an example of the therapeutic space enabling Pete to explore ideas about change – what did the right-hand part or the left-hand part of the forked track lead to? I would argue that my quietness and intensity of attunement to him helped him to create and then sustain these ideas – in other words, I was concentrated on facilitating the process of play itself at this point in the session rather than interpreting the content. The way that this process took place was an aspect of the uniqueness of the present relationship that had developed between us. It was the outcome and accumulation of the particular interactions that had taken place between us in the past, particularly the times when he had briefly felt himself to be alone in the presence of the therapist. This idea expands Winnicott's ideas about play and the capacity to be alone (Winnicott 1958).

I am realising more and more that this is a pivotal therapeutic experience that is particularly pertinent for children who are 'looked after', who in reality, for large stretches in their lives, are often so terribly alone in their life experiences. I am aware that I am making an important distinction between feeling lonely and isolated and the capacity to be alone, which I will try to clarify. Clinically, I am distinguishing between those times when children like Sammy and Pete feel intensely lonely and on their own in the world, and those times when they feel there is someone else with them, but in a way that is both with them but separate from them. I am referring to a transitional experience here because I am not describing someone else playing *with* the child. I am describing a child playing *because of* the presence of someone else who enables the child to dare to feel free enough and safe enough to play. This is an intermediate stage of play, in between the developmental stage where a baby is just starting to play, and the time when the same child is able to 'play on their own' without needing to have anyone else with him or her all the time.

This intermediate state of mind, in which there is the sense of not being entirely 'alone' while paradoxically feeling very alone and separate, is central to the experience of being alone in the presence of someone, which holds such therapeutic potential (Winnicott 1958). This experience is central to my thinking about enabling patients who find it very hard to play to start to play, and it is through this medium of play that the child becomes more able to express and work through his or her deepest anxieties.

Bowlby (1988: 151) had a similar concept of the therapeutic process when he said that he saw the therapeutic relationship as having

> the emphasis placed on the therapist's role as a companion for his patient in the latter's exploration of himself and his experiences, and less on the therapist's interpreting things to the patient. Whilst some traditional therapists might be described as adopting the stance 'I know, I'll tell you', the stance I advocate is one of 'You know, you tell me'.

To return to Pete's play with the train track. I eventually said that the little train might feel really scared that each time it came to the end of the track it would fall into the water. But then luckily, it seemed that some new track always arrived just in time. He had previously made a big play on the word 'now' – interspersing some of his play with 'now' this is happening, 'now' that – as if it was a new word for him. In this way, the immediacy of his sense of having to live in the present because he could not see the way ahead was powerfully conveyed. I pointed to the fork in the track with which he had been so engrossed and said that I thought he was trying to work out what it would mean to 'fork off' the track he was on with his foster parents and go on the other track with his mummy and daddy. It was as if he had run out of track with his foster parents and could go no further with them, but there was another route with his mummy and daddy, where there was lots of track. The trains needed a track and he needed a mummy and daddy. This was interpretative work, outside the transference, using the content of the play as a means of understanding his anxieties.

All of this was very moving – not least because Pete had found for himself the metaphor in his play, which I could not find in words. (Although I have not included it in this chapter, I had had a similar experience with Sammy – see Lanyado 1997, 1999a.) Following this session, I decided to buy Pete two more small wooden trains for his personal box of toys that he would not have to share with other patients, to deliberately represent his mummy and daddy. I wouldn't normally be so directive with a child, but the circumstances suggested that he might find this helpful and there was a time pressure to work as much as we could on these issues before he was introduced to his adoptive parents. Pete was delighted to have his own mummy and daddy trains and although this was clearly my idea and not his, he had the choice about whether or not to use his trains in the way that he did.

Pete spent the whole of the session playing with his mummy and daddy trains and the other shared trains on a track that he made up in sections, including (significantly) the fork in the track. I made very little comment during this play but again concentrated on facilitating the continuation of the play by remaining as close and attuned to him as possible. There was no longer any play about the train falling off the end of the track, but there were lots of couplings and uncouplings of the carriage to the different foster parent trains or the mummy and daddy trains, which I did eventually and briefly comment on to him. Again it was the intense concentration of this play and the fact that it was so sustained that was impressive in a little boy who prior to this had been so unable to settle to any sustained play. The little trains in his box meant a great deal to him, although he never wanted to take them home. They were a predominant theme in his play for the next two months during which time he met his adoptive parents and moved to live with them.

This was a very positive adoption to observe and Pete continued to come to therapy for two years after the period I have described. He did not have many other themes of play that were so sustained and important to him during therapy and he could often be boisterous, disruptive and unable to play. In his sessions this increased my feeling that the train play served a particular function in his therapy in helping him to think and feel about what it meant to go through the massive change of leaving his secure foster home to live with his adoptive parents. Interestingly, the only time that the train play reappeared after the sessions described was when Pete was approaching the end of his therapy – another important transition in his life. At this time, I was able to talk about his impending separation from me and how this revived feelings and memories of other separations, as well as rejections that he had experienced. When he was asked if there were any of the small toys from his box, just a few, that he might like to keep when his therapy came to an end, he chose the two little trains.

The tolerance of paradox and the creation of transitional phenomena during therapy

Transitional objects are first created under the pressure of needing to find a way to bridge two very different states of mind – such as sleep and waking, or mother's presence and mother's absence. The infant needs to find some way of negotiating the mental space that exists in between these experiences. What could entail more different and opposing states of mind than moving from one mother and father figure to another, externally and internally? Could this not also be the optimal emotional environment for the creation of new transitional objects, *if the prevailing conditions are right*? It was here that I feel that Sammy gave me a possible answer to my question about how best to help him at this momentous time in his life. Did my concentration on creating a therapeutic environment in which he could feel free to explore the space he found himself in enable him to find his own creative solutions which included the creation of new transitional phenomena?

There is no reason why new transitional objects and experiences should not develop at any stage of life where the paradoxes of change are foremost – for example, a particular tune, or item of clothing or smell that takes on a helpful meaning when changing jobs, ending a relationship or going through the acute stages of mourning. It could be argued that the emergence of new transitional phenomena within therapy as well as outside it is entirely in keeping with the whole process of enabling patients to live more creatively. The extension of transitional phenomena to the whole field of cultural experience – music, art, dance, religious experience and so on – is an important part of Winnicott's thesis about transitional phenomena (Winnicott 1951). As adults we are likely to express this creativity through broader cultural interests and a greater sense of psychic freedom. Children are more likely to express this increased creativity through freer play and the creation of new transitional objects and phenomena as appropriate to their stage of development.

Where there has been severe early emotional deprivation, such as is often the case with children who have been taken into care, the child may well not have experienced the facilitating environment during early childhood within which transitional phenomena might be created. This is just one of the many developmental losses these children experience, in this case a loss which might in some measure have helped in coping with more ordinary anxiety as well as traumatic experience. Tragically, where there has been a transitional object, such as a special teddy or blanket, it has often been lost as children in care move from one placement to another.

The hypothesis that I am putting forward is that therapy may have facilitated the creation of new and pertinent transitional phenomena, which helped Sammy and Pete to bear to exist in the paradoxical emotional space in their minds and hearts between their respective foster and adoptive families.

The paradox of leaving the security of a foster family who have helped a child so much, and moving to the unknown adoptive family, requires that the child remain in touch with painful feelings of separation and loss while remaining open to the exciting possibilities of a home where he or she can stay 'for ever'. The wish to manically run to a 'happy-ever-after' solution of the child's problems is powerfully present in the professional system of adults looking after the child, as well as at times in the child and adoptive family. If these feelings predominate, the intense pain of anticipatory mourning as well as, when the time comes, real mourning of the foster family, may be denied, fudged or even overlooked in a manner that denies the child's psychic reality. As already discussed, the ability to experience the sadness of loss and mourning is likely to be severely impaired in children such as these, and highly defended against. Even in children who are less emotionally disadvantaged, endings can be difficult.

The child and adoptive family may reject the previously valued (by the child) foster family, or wish to draw a line between themselves and the child's painful past. While understandable, this effectively cuts the child off from a large part of him or herself, which cannot augur well for the adoptive family's long-term future. These defences can moderate with time, but it is clearly valuable to try to help the child and the adoptive family to remain as undefended as possible to the painfulness of all the difficult feelings that they are trying to digest during the upheaval of the early days of the adoption.

Another commonly observed difficulty is that the pain of parting from the foster family may be so intense that the child, family, fostering social workers and at times the therapist, can be out of touch with the tremendous need in the child to feel wanted 'for ever' and to belong to a family of his or her own. Foster families offer the most extraordinary emotional gifts to the children they succeed in caring for, in the way that Sammy had been cared for. And then they have to let go of the child into whom they have invested so much emotional energy. For the child, the foster family has offered a vital transitional and paradoxical experience in which he or she is both in the heart of the family and yet not fully a part of it. When the pain of the loss of this good experience with the foster family can be stayed with, the move to the adoptive family may potentially be experienced in a less defensive, more alive, but of course at the time more painful, way. The capacity to tolerate this transition and paradox will be enhanced by the manner in which the foster family have both taken the child to heart and yet not, in the final analysis, taken the child fully into the family.

The evident sadness of the foster family in saying goodbye was clearly recognised by Sammy when he repeatedly asked his foster mother, close to the time of leaving her, whether she would cry when he went. She often told him that she thought all the family would cry – as indeed they did. He needed to know that his sadness at parting from her was both understandable and reciprocated. As for many looked after children, so often in the past, relief, anger and rejection had typified his 'goodbyes'. Enabling the child to mourn the loss of the foster family *and* welcome the new beginning and feel excited about becoming part of the adoptive family, requires that the therapist tolerates this paradox and maintains a balanced perspective on the child's life situation. This is required both within the total therapeutic relationship and within the communications that take place during this crucial time in the professional network of adults surrounding the child, as well as with the foster and adoptive families.

The pieces of paper that preceded Sammy's use of the green ball, as well as the green ball itself, indicated that Sammy was finding psychic ways of bridging the gap between being with me and being without me, when he said goodbye at the end of the session. I think that it can be argued that he extended this new ability to the whole process of saying goodbye to his foster family, while saying hello to his adoptive family.

Thinking about Pete's play, I think it can be seen that while the trains did not become transitional objects in the clear sense that the green ball was for Sammy, they had great significance for Pete. They helped him to cope with the many conflicting and paradoxical feelings that he was only dimly aware of, because of his massive defences against psychic pain. But interestingly, it was these trains that he took with him when his therapy ended. Thinking about this now, I almost feel that during the time that the adoption took place, Pete felt that he had no rights over anything or anyone, just as he never thought that he would have a mummy and daddy. However, by the end of therapy this feeling had completely changed, as he increasingly felt that he finally belonged to someone; indeed, belonged to a family.

Pete was not in torment during the period of transition from fostering to adoption in the way that Sammy was. But he was distinctly puzzled and more uncomfortable internally than he was used to being. I think he could be described as experiencing what Stern (1985) describes as a 'sense of emergent self' – something inside him that was in the process of significant change. Whether it was Sammy's passionate nature which led to his attachment to the ball, while Pete's defensive nature did not allow this level of engagement with the trains, is open to debate. However, I think that Pete's intense play with the trains and Sammy's use of the ball in both instances helped them to cope with the paradox of the extraordinary changes in their lives. They were different types of transitional phenomena serving the same function.

A further transitional space

There is a further intermediate space which exists between external and internal reality, which the therapist must carefully consider when working with children who are 'looked after' by the local authority. This intermediate space relates to the manner in which the therapist communicates and actively engages with the adults in the child's life, as well as with the child's internal world as seen in the kind of play described above. The need to face in two directions at once and wisely hold this position serves several important functions when offering psychotherapy to children in transition from fostering to adoption.

In ideal circumstances, just as with other children in therapy, there will be a co-worker in the multidisciplinary team working closely with the child's parents/carers as well as, where necessary, communicating with other professionals involved with the child. In this model, the psychotherapist is freed to concentrate on the child's inner world, while knowing about but not engaging with the child's external world, through appropriate communication with the co-worker who works with the external world. There may be situations in which the therapist meets with parents or other important adults in the child's life, in which case great care will be taken to work out appropriate boundaries and areas of confidentiality.

Some would argue that this model is not appropriate for all children – for example, when working with young children under 5, or with children with autism or psychosis, and that there may be clinical situations where it is essential for the therapist to have regular therapeutic contact with the parents or carers as well as the child. Current practice across Europe in work with parents is interestingly illustrated in Tsiantis *et al.* (2000). As psychotherapists widen the range of children to whom they offer treatment, there are many variations in the degree to which they work with the child's external world, and there may well be many differing views about how to approach each individual case.

Children who are 'looked after' live within an extremely complex network of adult relationships. It is not unusual to hear of children who have contact with their birth family, live in a foster family and are in the process of being adopted by a third family. Each of these families will have different social workers working with them, and there may well be an adoption agency and allocated social worker involved in the process. The child may also be attending school or an educational unit, and may additionally at times have medical problems. Unfortunately, the people in this network often change jobs, or are under enormous pressure because they are responsible for many other children like the one the therapist is working with. The potential for chaotic management of crucial events in the child's life is enormous. Even where there is reasonable constancy within the network, the potential for conflict over what is best for the child is huge, not only because of straightforward differences of opinion, but also because of the projections of painful feelings of loss, anger, rejection, disappointment, abuse – the list is long – that become lodged in the system and the individuals who are trying to work within it. When things go wrong, or there is disagreement about what is in the child's best interests, it is easy for blame to be allocated to others in the system, where in fact the 'blame' (if it can be called that) resides within the difficulties in the organisational dynamics of the system itself. It can be argued that the needs of the child in these circumstances are best met by offering consultancy to the system itself, or certain parts of it, and that working in a more separate way with the child alone is counterproductive (Sprince 2000, 2002).

However, in keeping with the theme of this chapter, I would argue that an intermediate view is possible and particularly valuable because of the nature of offering psychotherapy in transitions. Even where there is good co-working in the team, and particularly where this is not possible, I think that the therapist's active representation of the child's anxieties, defences and conflicts within the planning for the actual transition can be extremely valuable. The degree of the psychotherapist's involvement in meetings depends on what kind of co-working is possible. However, I think that at the outset of the treatment it has to be clearly established with the social workers responsible for the child's care plan that the clinic/psychotherapist must be consulted and involved at all the key stages of the transition process. This does not of course mean that the psychotherapist should make the decisions that only the social workers can make. However, it does mean that every effort should be made to ensure that those decisions that have to be made are as well informed as is possible about how the child currently feels and is likely to cope with the plans that are under consideration.

However, it is important to stress that there is no single way of working that is being advocated here. Each patient and the network that surrounds him or her has to be thought about individually according to the child's current situation, whenever work with the network is considered. Some patients at certain points in their therapy might feel betrayed by the therapist going to a meeting about them, and the therapist might or might not decide to go to the meeting and work with whatever the consequences of this decision might be. In other situations, a patient might feel that the therapist lets him or her down by *not* being at a crucial meeting, and representing his or her needs. Great sensitivity is required in making these decisions. Frequently there are disadvantages as well as advantages involved in all such decisions and the therapist has to weigh up what in effect is the 'lesser of two evils' in deciding on the wisest course of action.

My point is that contact with the adults in the child's life for children who are 'looked after' may necessarily have to be greater than with children living in less complex situations. This has consequences for children who have good reason not to trust adults, who may fear that the adult will betray them, or not respect vital aspects of their privacy. Depending on the age of the child, these concerns need to be addressed openly in the therapy as well as the difficulties resulting from these concerns being expressed to the adults working in the network around the child.

For example, I did not need to have a co-worker for Sammy because the fostering social worker who had worked within an interdisciplinary team in the past was able to be so effective in his work with the foster families. This meant that I could be confident in his understanding of the therapeutic process and the support that his work gave to the therapy. However, I still made an active contribution to the discussions that took place about what kind of family might be best for Sammy and whether there were any serious drawbacks to the family who were eventually put forward to the adoption panel. When the family was approved, I met with the adoptive parents to talk to them about the child they were adopting. The extent of my work with the networks around Sammy and Pete may well have been a reflection of their young age. With older children this would have been more complicated.

The actual process of how Sammy first met his adoptive parents, and then their extended families, was also discussed in detail with me, as was the first visit that he made to his adoptive home and his first overnight stay. The importance of this attention to detail during the introduction of the child to the adoptive family cannot be stressed enough. This parallels the attention to detail that new parents give to their newborn baby, the primary parental preoccupation (to extend Winnicott's 1956 concept of primary maternal preoccupation) that is so essential to the baby getting into the parents' minds. During the crucial few weeks that the child is living the transition from fostering to adoption, he or she needs to be very firmly in the minds of all the professionals involved in the process. The child's therapist is particularly well placed to facilitate this process and to present a model of the kind of detail that needs to be thought about. The experience of baby observation is particularly useful when trying to help all the professionals involved to understand why this level of absorption by all involved is so valuable. The process I am describing is a mix between consultation to the system from within it, and communication about the nature of the child's inner world. The therapist might also benefit from the opportunity to discuss with an experienced colleague the complicated process he or she is part of and yet trying to observe and consult to.

One of the main aims of being so involved in the child's outside world at this particular time, which can feel very fraught to all involved (not unlike a group of midwives trying to attend a difficult labour), is to try to minimise potentially difficult and distressing arrangements – which can seem like a good idea at the time. For example, it had been agreed that the first time Sammy's parents went to his school would be on the afternoon of his sports day. Everyone seemed to have forgotten that Sammy's difficulty with not winning (that is, with being the 'loser') could turn him into an angry and desperate child at the best of times. Sports day was likely to be difficult enough as it was without adding the presence of his adoptive parents to this already tricky situation.

The tendency to repeat traumatic incidents, and particularly traumatic endings, from the past can be powerfully and unconsciously present within the network of professionals. This determined return of destructive processes in the midst of such a delicate transition requires vigilance in the professional network so that they can stop the powerful process of repeating the traumatic past from being acted out again in the present. During the transition, many defences are raised in the professionals themselves, and as already discussed there can be a resulting insensitivity to both the extremes of distress that can emerge in the child, and the great excitement that can also be present. The feelings that emerge can be close to intolerable to inexperienced or vulnerable social workers and foster carers, and denial or impatience with the feelings that the child expresses can easily arise.

I have gone into such detail about the complexity of what is happening in the child's external world because I believe that this is one of the clinical situations where, *temporarily*, the psychotherapist must tolerate and indeed encourage more than the usual osmosis in his or her mind between the child's external and the internal world. The therapy sessions need to be well informed about the day-to-day progress of the 'introductions' and all the successes and difficulties that have been encountered. Similarly, the professional network needs to be well informed by the therapist as well as the foster parents and adoptive parents about how well the child is coping with the strains of the situation, so that if need be the process can be speeded up or slowed down in tune with the child's ability to cope. The meaning of all that is happening externally, as it is experienced within the child's internal world, needs to be responded to as sensitively as possible.

A pragmatism and readiness to engage with the child's reality becomes paramount for a short while. While much of this can be conveyed through a good co-worker, the actual physical presence of the therapist at key points during the process is more likely to lead to an active wish in the adoptive parents to accept offers of further therapeutic work, than if the therapist is experienced as too much on the outside of the drama of the transition. Even if the current therapist is not able for practical reasons to continue the therapy when the child moves to the adoptive home, the adoptive parents are likely to be more open to asking for help in the future, or accepting referral at the time to other therapeutic resources, if their experience of the therapist at the time of the transition is a helpful one.

Holding this tension and being prepared to enter into the experience of the transition itself is a question of technique during the session, as well as containment of anxiety, and sensitivity to defensiveness within the network. It could be said that during the transition – which in my experience tends to last for two to four weeks – the child ideally needs to be 'in the pocket' of all the adults in the network in such a way that he or she is accompanied as best as possible through this incredible process. The recognition of the interdependence of internal and external reality, particularly during such massive changes in the child's external world, places a pressure on the therapist to similarly venture into the transitional space where anything can happen, and the therapeutic task is to try to ensure that the outcome is as creative as possible.

Chapter 7

The story of Lot's wife: the importance of the therapist's 'personal signature' at times of critical change[1]

Moments of spontaneity and other unusual clinical events which might, however briefly, reveal the nature of the therapist's personal thoughts and feelings, can often be viewed as breaches of technique and the boundaries of therapy. The therapist may feel that more of his or her private self than is advisable has come through the consulting room door and intruded on the session, and of course there are times when this may well be the case. However, there are other times when this kind of experience proves to be surprisingly productive of positive change, suggesting that these unusual and disconcerting experiences need to be understood in a different and more positive therapeutic and theoretical light (Symington 1986; Carlberg 1997; Stern *et al.* 1998).

This chapter describes some unusual clinical events that took place during a period of crisis in the treatment of Hilary, a suicidal adolescent girl, which seemed to be helpful in keeping her safe during this time. The once-weekly treatment lasted for nine months, and for a good deal of this time I had to work extremely carefully with her as I did not feel that she was sufficiently held outside the sessions to allow me to interpret other than with great caution. Her treatment with me ended when she was admitted to a therapeutic unit where she was able to have intensive psychotherapy and explore the depths that I felt I had to leave alone while I was working with her.

Her therapy during this period between living at home in considerable danger of killing herself, and seeing her safely admitted to the therapeutic unit, very literally saw her through a vital transition in her life. Hilary had all the hallmarks of someone who was stuck in a very dangerous place but was terrified of moving into a freer but unknown space. Even when she started to make this move, which she found terrifying, I often felt that she was stuck in quicksand and rapidly being sucked under, unable to move

---

1 This chapter is based on the 2001b paper, 'The symbolism of the story of Lot and his wife: the function of the "present relationship" and non-interpretative aspects of the therapeutic relationship in facilitating change', *Journal of Child Psychotherapy*, 27(1): 19–33.

either forwards or backwards. This made me feel that I had to keep throwing her lifelines in a way that I have rarely done with other patients. Was this acting out in the transference? Was it vital for her survival? Or was this a situation in which my 'personal signature' as a therapeutic tool was required in these dire circumstances?

At the time, I found myself 'being' and behaving in Hilary's treatment in ways that were unusual because I felt that this was necessary to keep her alive. I suspect, and in some cases know, that many of my colleagues have taken similar measures – with suicidal patients as well as with other patients who are at crucial junctures in their lives. These measures are often introduced in clinical discussion with phrases such as 'I'm not sure if I should have done this, but . . .' What tends to follow is (surprisingly often, to any non-psychoanalytic observer) an account of some form of more personal and humane intervention which the therapist fears has breached the boundary of therapeutic neutrality and exposed the therapist's ordinary human response to the patient. Sometimes these are spontaneous acts; sometimes they are more carefully thought out strategies that go further than usual in exposing the therapist's personal self and which involve a therapeutic 'risk' on the therapist's part. My decision to allow Sammy to take the green ball home in the last chapter and my decision to buy the 'mummy and daddy trains' for Pete, were in this category. The decisions in these instances were based on my perception that 'something more' than what I usually offered in therapy was required at these critical times in the patients' lives.

It interests me that more often than not these types of unusual clinical event, that require careful thought and monitoring after they have happened, do not prove, in the main, to be a disastrous form of acting out on the therapist's part. There is something to learn from this about the total therapeutic relationship. Indeed, surprisingly often, events such as these seem to deepen and hold the therapeutic process when it is under great pressure. Carpy discusses these issues and comes to the conclusion that experiencing and tolerating the patient's projections in the counter-transference inevitably involves some partial acting out. He sees this as an 'unavoidable aspect of the situation which in the end is of positive therapeutic value' (1989: 289). I would argue that these spontaneous (and in reality usually mildly personal) revealing events in therapy face us with an aspect of our work that we have tended to overlook, take for granted or undervalue.

Psychoanalytic discomfort with acknowledging how important the actual person of the therapist is seems to be located in fears that this may encourage the therapist to see him or herself as the good or even the ideal object and to become blind to the negative transference. There is always the potential for the ego, with a capital E, of the therapist to become much too present in the therapy. However, this is one of many risks that need to be monitored by the therapist in his or her self-scrutiny, as well as in ongoing professional development such as supervision or indeed ongoing personal therapy. The dangers inherent in the therapist behaving in ways that he or she perceives to be 'good' parenting of the patient and the psychoanalytic history of these concerns are discussed in the context of the dangers of offering corrective emotional experience by Baker (1993).

However, to counter these real concerns, many therapists would point out that within the clear boundaries of the therapeutic setting as generally accepted today therapists inevitably, as a part of the process, provide an experience which counteracts or neutralises distressing emotional interactions in the patient's past and present. The reliability and consistency of the therapeutic setting, the way in which the therapist listens to and thinks about the patient, the careful preparation and thought that goes into work around the separations in therapy – all these aspects of therapy that are intrinsic to psychoanalytic therapy in themselves often provide a very different experience from that which the patient may have previously experienced.

The importance of Stern *et al.*'s. ideas about moments-of-meeting and the 'personal signature of the therapist' were discussed at the start of this book and there are examples of these concepts in action in the consulting room throughout (*Infant Mental Health Journal* 1998; Stern *et al.* 1998). In the context of this chapter I want to enlarge further on these ideas as well as think about whether the 'presence' of the therapist is different to the therapist's 'personal signature'.

Stern *et al.* (1998) argue that moments-of-meeting are the something more than interpretation that makes the patient-therapist communication authentic, providing an important vehicle of psychic change. They describe moments-of-meeting as being the culmination of a process entailing a combination of 'moving along', 'present moments' and 'now' moments. They argue that, during these moments 'The therapist must use a specific aspect of his/her individuality that carries a personal signature. The two are meeting as persons relatively unhidden by their usual therapeutic roles, for that moment' (p. 913). Note the word 'must' in this sentence – the implication is that this is a very deliberate and even necessary action by the therapist. It is not a purely spontaneous act, although the feelings in the therapist that prompt the use of the personal signature are presumably sufficiently strong to make the therapist move out of his or her usual way of being with the patient for that moment. The meeting of two 'persons relatively unhidden by their usual therapeutic roles' (Stern *et al.* 1998: 913) takes place in an instant which is close to spontaneous, but I think it is based on unconscious and conscious perceptions that have been taking place between patient and therapist for a good while before this in therapy. This ongoing experience, the gradual overlap of the therapist's and patient's reverie or play, together with the many small experiences of being alone in the presence of the therapist, leading to the gradual emergence of the transitional space, sets the scene for the moment-of-meeting when the therapist's signature is briefly evident.

In the language of developmental psychology, Stern *et al.* argue that moments-of-meeting take place within the 'shared implicit relationship' which grows as a result of the attunement between therapist and patient. This attunement develops during therapy and is based on minute interactions in the domain of intersubjectivity in which there is a more or less accurate sensing of the therapist's and patient's person. Stern *et al.* argue that it is in the times that surround these moments-of-meeting that crucial therapeutic changes take place. This is a very radical deduction to emerge from the deliberations within this group, which is studying the process of change. It is important to bear in mind that these moments-of-meeting are indeed moments, and that the more ordinary processes of 'going-on-being' resume after these moments – although Stern *et al.* argue that the change brought about by a moment-of-meeting alters the mental landscape from which the patient now operates.

It is difficult to capture these experiences in words, and what tends to happen is something closer to an impressionistic painting rather than a portrait of the experiences that are under discussion. Clinical material helps to paint the picture.

'In my pocket': the psychological 'carrying' of a suicidal patient

During the time that Hilary was particularly stuck and unable to contemplate any change in her life other than death, the biblical story of Lot and his wife kept coming into my therapeutic reverie. This story vividly captures the image of what happens when a family is faced with the prospect of dramatic change. The story is rich in allegory, but I shall concentrate on the aspects that relate to the risks and dangers of change, as opposed to the attractions of staying the same, however fraught or dangerous that may also be. In the Bible story we are told that Lot and his family were the only people that the angels of God considered to be good and worth saving out of all the citizens of the wicked city of Sodom that God had commanded them to destroy. The angels warned Lot and his family that they must flee the city immediately. It was an act of faith that they decided to leave, making themselves homeless and facing an unknown and possibly dangerous future. Not all the family left. Lot's sons-in-law did not take the angels' warning seriously, so only Lot, his wife and their two daughters left the city, and then with some understandable trepidation. The angels also warned Lot and his family that they must not look back at the burning city, but must keep on walking away from it into the plains and eventually into the mountains, however treacherous this path may be.

However, Lot's wife could not resist the temptation to look back and was turned into a pillar of salt. Lot and his daughters did not look back, but journeyed onwards and survived despite all the hardships that followed.

While working with Hilary this story was often in my thoughts as it so vividly depicts the tremendous risks and anxieties that surround this kind of 'before and after' change. I should like to suggest that, when we are faced with a patient who is finding it enormously difficult, painful and terrifying to change, it is the 'personal signature' of our work which pulls the therapy – and of course the patient – through. Going forward, staying in the present and leaving the often traumatic past behind is very frightening and requires courage and determination. I believe that at the crucial point of change, when some new response or behaviour *has* to happen or there will be *no* change, it is within the present relationship that we hold and carry our patients through this frightening but potentially hopeful passage in their lives. In particular, at times of clear crisis, I think that therapists often take the risk of using their personal signature because, with the gathering of clinical experience of this kind, they intuitively know that 'something more' is required of them at this critical moment, to help their patient through. Stern *et al.* (1998: 912) describe this vividly as follows:

> These moments are pregnant with an unknown future that can feel like an impasse or an opportunity. The present becomes very dense sub-jectively as in a 'moment of truth' . . . The application of habitual technical moves will not suffice. The analyst intuitively recognises that a window of opportunity for some kind of therapeutic reorganisation or derailment is present, and the patient may recognise that he has arrived at a watershed in the therapeutic relationship.

Hilary had been in once-weekly therapy for only a few weeks when she began to share with me the suicidal ruminations that dominated her mind. These happened particularly at night, when she would regularly cut her arms and stomach to try to ease her distress. After much difficulty, she had been persuaded to come for help by a teacher who had noticed the scars on her arms. She was constantly preoccupied with thoughts about taking tablets or how to get hold of knives and razors so that she could kill herself. Alarmingly, she claimed that her parents were oblivious to her suicidal thoughts and intentions, and she absolutely refused to let the clinic have any contact with them about this, as she did not want them to know how she felt.

When I discussed this very worrying situation with my colleagues in the clinic team, it was felt that, on balance and in view of the fact that Hilary was over 16, and as it had been so hard to engage her in treatment, it was wiser to respect her strongly-held wishes that we should not contact her parents. She had made it very clear that she would break off therapy if we did not respect what she felt. Hilary was not behaving hysterically and was a high achiever. I feared that, if she carried through any of her suicide plans, she was likely to succeed in killing herself.

Hilary could give no particular reason or trauma to which she linked her suicidal wishes and I felt that trying to probe this in any way was dangerous and intrusive during the early days of treatment. Although I did try to gently explore these feelings, Hilary did not see that there was any point in this. As a result I came to the conclusion that therapeutic priorities seemed to demand that I pay acute and intense attention to her perilous state of mind, rather than search for some understanding or insight into her self-destructive thoughts, feelings and behaviour. She was a clear suicidal risk, and the clinic's problem was how to get her to a place of safety within which she might dare to try to make more sense of her self-destructive feelings. Although no one else in the clinic was allowed by Hilary to be involved, I was fortunately well supported by my colleagues throughout her therapy.

It gradually became apparent to me during this early period of treatment that there was a small part of Hilary which was signalling to me from behind the massively self-destructive aspect of herself that dominated our sessions, and this part wanted help to stay alive. Horne (2001) has written about these 'brief communications from the edge' in her work with an adolescent patient who was antisocial and at risk of becoming sexually abusive. It was vital that I kept looking out for these very faint and hesitant 'brief communications'. My intense awareness of having to be highly alert to these signs contrasted strikingly with Hilary's description of how her parents were apparently completely unaware of her distraught state of mind. Hilary was incredibly good at deliberately concealing what she felt, while her parents seemed to have great difficulty receiving and processing her desperate non-verbal communications. Her arms were by this point obviously scarred from her cutting and she was adding fresh wounds nightly – according to Hilary, without her parents noticing.

Hilary was seeing her GP, ostensibly for treatment of a completely separate medical problem, but was able to tell me at the end of a very worrying session that he also knew about how deeply depressed she was and had sensibly prescribed, and was carefully monitoring, some anti-depressant medication. However, when I asked whether I could contact her GP to alert him to her suicidal ruminations, she absolutely refused to let me do so. Again, following discussion with colleagues, it was felt that on balance I would have to hold this anxiety and could not contact the GP without Hilary's permission. This kind of difficult judgement is much easier for the therapist to live with when made together with colleagues. The balance of preserving the confidentiality of the child or adolescent patient, while keeping him or her safe, is precarious at times and decisions often have to be made on the side of the lesser of two evils. As with the work with the network of professionals surrounding children who are 'looked after', or living in a therapeutic community, there are many factors to be taken into account. All of these factors will be highly individualised according to the patient, the particular phase of therapy and the issue itself.

I was unable to offer more than once-weekly sessions to Hilary, and even if I had she may well have not taken this up. So, in an attempt to hold the situation as well as I could, I encouraged Hilary to write to me between sessions. If she did not actually have time to send the letters before the session, she was to bring them with her. We read and talked about her writings during the sessions. I told her that I would keep her and her letters 'in my pocket' – and I literally did carry her letters with me as well as hold her very actively in my mind and heart during this time. I also told her that the clinic secretaries would contact me immediately if she phoned and wanted to have a word with me between sessions.

This activity was fuelled by my experience that interpretations about Hilary's need and wish to experience my aroused anxiety and attention to her were dismissed as meaningless. She so genuinely believed that she was a worthless person that what I said meant nothing to her. She needed the evidence of some actions on my part that demonstrated that I felt her life was worth living. In Carpy's terms, this could be seen as a partial acting out which was ultimately therapeutic (1989).

During the next six weeks this very worrying stalemate continued. Then, almost in passing, Hilary mentioned that her GP had suggested that she be referred to an adult psychiatrist as she was nearly 18 and likely to need ongoing treatment. She asked me, in a frightened but surprisingly wistful way, whether this would mean admission to hospital. This was a new and vital clue to what she wanted. Until this point, she had felt that there were only two options: denying that there was any problem to her parents and continuing her suffering, or killing herself. A third option had now arrived: the possibility of being admitted to a local adult psychiatric hospital. I have to say that this was not an option that I had thought a real possibility until this time.

I immediately explored the idea of a referral to an adult psychiatrist with Hilary and she finally agreed to me having contact with her GP. This was an important and moving breakthrough and at the end of the session I found myself very deliberately patting her arm in appreciation of what this meant for her. I also felt tearful after the session, and very relieved. Looking back, I am sure that Hilary was subliminally aware of the struggle that had gone on in the therapeutic relationship up to this point to persuade her to take hold of the lifelines that I was throwing her, as well as my genuine worry about her. I think she was probably also aware of my relief that she was finally able to take this first small step towards safety. There was no disguising this and, thinking in terms of moments-of-meeting, possibly the authenticity of what we both saw through the 'window of opportunity' that briefly appeared during the session may well have been what helped her to take this step.

I spoke to the GP and he arranged an urgent appointment for Hilary with the adult psychiatrist. By her next session, Hilary was seriously able to consider becoming a voluntary patient at the local psychiatric hospital. She had somehow (I was never told how) managed to talk about this with her family and spontaneously mentioned someone she knew of who had gone on from the mental hospital to a long-term therapeutic unit. She was admitted to the local psychiatric acute ward a few days later and I was able to liaise with the psychiatrist in charge of the ward to arrange to carry on seeing Hilary once a week during her stay. Hilary received humane and sensitive nursing care in this unit, which was not particularly psycho-dynamically inclined. In many ways, as well as monitoring her medication and safety, the unit provided a refuge for her, within which she could feel safer than she had felt for a long time – but her suicidal ruminations continued.

Throughout the time that I saw Hilary in hospital we were able to have a private room in which to meet at a regular time for her sessions. I maintained the psychoanalytic work with her within the sessions and felt safer to interpret in the transference and to talk about her relationships with her parents. I also kept in regular phone contact with the psychiatrist and senior nurses, and the application for Hilary's placement at an adolescent unit was a joint one. My work in therapeutic units helped me greatly to find constructive ways of making these links with the hospital.

I do not normally make it so clear to patients that they matter to me and it is not necessary for most patients to be shown this in the way that I felt I had to show Hilary, if she was to stay alive. While other patients might occasionally write letters or poetry in between sessions, I would not normally tell them that I would (and did) keep their letters with me and that they would be 'in my pocket'. During the time that Hilary was in the psychiatric hospital, I phoned her quite regularly between sessions for a brief word and to show that she was truly on my mind.

I did all these atypical things in this treatment, not because I wanted to be a heroic rescuer or out of a sense of my own self-importance, but because of the extent of the responsibility that I felt to keep Hilary alive by holding her in every way I could think of between sessions. While she was well cared for in the hospital, Hilary could at times be very adept at inducing a state of inattentiveness in the staff, a transference phenomenon in which the staff inadvertently became out of touch with Hilary's suicidal ruminations in the way that Hilary's parents had been. When this was evident in our sessions, once-weekly therapy felt woefully inadequate and the gaps between sessions enormous. I would always tell the staff of my concern and they were appropriately responsive as a result. However, I felt that, particularly at these times, Hilary needed evidence that she was really in my mind when I was not with her. I should emphasise that she was not a patient who attempted to endear herself to anyone. Additionally, while she was more positive than she had been, her treatment and therapy throughout this period simultaneously remained full of anger and resentment towards the hospital staff and myself for not letting her kill herself.

Was I overreacting and totally out of role, or was I using the strength of our present relationship and my personal signature to help Hilary not to 'look back' as Lot's wife had done and to keep going along the dangerous and difficult path she now found herself on? I asked myself and colleagues this question frequently during this phase of the treatment and still believe I was not rationalising inappropriate behaviour on my part.

During Hilary's time in the psychiatric hospital she was often in serious danger of turning back and abandoning her efforts to change and find a way of living. She still spent most of her waking hours thinking about how she could kill herself. Fortunately, the staff on the ward were increasingly vigilant to signals of suicidal risk and they carried Hilary through in a very practical way during this time. She was astonished to find (and was able to verbalise this in therapy) that, as she put it, 'Somehow they know when I'm about to do something to myself, like cut myself, and they just appear out of nowhere. How do they know?' This was a genuine discovery for her, that someone could know how she was feeling without her needing to say anything. Within her relationship with her parents it was by now painfully apparent to the staff in the hospital that her non-verbal communications and emotional needs were almost completely unmet.

One can certainly postulate that Hilary's mother was depressed or possibly lacked the capacity to receive and process her baby's non-verbal communications from the start of life – some of her other children had had serious problems in their development. Hilary's intelligence and capacity to hide her true self behind a high-achieving but essentially false self had given her mother a sense that she could be a good mother after all (Miller 1987) – hence Hilary's desperate but eventually doomed attempts to pretend to her parents that all was well. But this was deeply inauthentic.

In addition to this, I always felt that the extraordinary level of what felt, at times, like blindness in this mother to her daughter's acute distress had, in unconscious fantasy, a murderous quality to it. This made me wonder whether her mother had tried to abort Hilary but failed. While this was consciously unknown to Hilary, in the ongoing relationship with her mother it was unconsciously but constantly being acted out in Hilary's powerful preoccupations with killing herself and feeling she had no right to live. On a conscious level, Hilary and her mother appeared to be very close and no doubt would have been horrified had there been any awareness of this possible underlying dynamic.

When Hilary was in hospital and at her worst, in great emotional pain and unable to decide whether or not to apply for a place at the therapeutic unit, I found myself talking to her very quietly about the fact that while it was agonisingly difficult for her to live, it was also more difficult than she had previously believed to die. She was very stuck in her treatment at this time and still risked becoming immobilised and unable to continue to change (turned into a lifeless pillar of salt?) because her difficulties in letting go of the past were so entrenched within her ruminations about her lack of self-worth. It was not until long after her treatment ended that I connected this interpretation with my (and her?) unspoken fantasy that her mother may have tried to kill her *in utero*, but had been unable to. Hilary had a stronger life force in her than she really wished at times, which stopped her from killing herself however terribly she was suffering at the time. This was a paradox that she ultimately had to learn to live with.

Well on into her treatment in the therapeutic unit, in addition to other significant traumatic factors, Hilary learnt from her mother that she had indeed been the result of an unplanned and unwanted pregnancy. This had been preserved as a family secret that her siblings and parents of course knew about, but Hilary (consciously) did not. Whether her mother really had tried to abort her remains unknown. However, the intensity of the efforts of the staff in the adult psychiatric unit and the therapeutic unit to keep Hilary alive, as well as my own efforts, must have related to the side of her that needed to feel that her life was important to others. She found this genuinely astonishing each time she had evidence of it.

Some further thoughts

While Hilary could be thought of as being a 'borderline' patient, which could account for some of what I perceived as her need to have concrete evidence of our relationship, she actually functioned (ostensibly) remarkably well at times in the outside world. I cannot therefore justify my intuitive wish to provide concrete evidence of our relationship purely on the basis that she was significantly out of touch with reality or unable to symbolise. Rather, I find myself thinking in terms of *stages* of internalisation, containment and treatment. There was much evidence in the transference, as well as in the hospital staff's observation of Hilary's actual relationship with her parents, that projective and introjective communication was very poorly developed between them. Hilary, being a gifted child in Miller's (1987) sense, had managed to survive by eliciting responsive relationships, particularly from the school staff who knew her, as well as other adults that she came into contact with. Simultaneously she presented a false and inauthentic self to the rest of the world, including her parents, in which she looked as if all was well. These means of survival were breaking down when she entered therapy.

Perhaps it was because of the need to demonstrate authenticity within the therapeutic relationship that I felt the need to 'show' more of myself in what I offered to Hilary than I do with most other patients. She simply did not believe that her feelings and anxieties could be communicated without words and received, and my actions were possibly the only way, at this stage in her emotional life, that she might feel that she had any evidence which might persuade her otherwise. It is possible that my actions were an enactment of the projection-introjection cycle described by Bion (1962a, 1962b), which, it could be argued, for some patients may be the precursor of the mentalisation of this process. It may be necessary to provide a modeling of this process at a concrete level before patients such as Hilary can develop a mental representation of it. In such circumstances, this enactment might be necessary to provide the rudiments of containment, before the mental processes are fully developed.

The core question I am raising is whether the unusual aspects of my way of working with Hilary, where my personal signature was particularly evident, enabled her to keep on walking away from her deadly internal hell, despite the emotional perils that lay ahead of her. Prior to the session in which she very tentatively hinted that referral to the psychiatric hospital could be a desperate but nevertheless authentic way of staying alive, she had been able to own only a tiny part of this aspect of herself. Until this time it had largely resided in those around her who had been able to receive this very heavily disguised projection.

The powerful impact that Hilary had on all the professionals, including me, who tried so hard to help her was the result of projective identification. However, drawing on this experience, there could have been several ways of responding. It can be argued that my openly expressed wish that I wanted to help her to live (verbally and through my actions) was a therapeutic enactment which took place within the present relationship between us. As her therapist, trying to help her to choose life with all its pains and difficulties, I was responding from within our present relationship which had not become contaminated with fantasies of maternal murderousness on my part and the dangers of acting this out in some way within the transference. The fact that this was so is interesting in itself. My work with Hilary lasted for only nine months and served the particular function of trying to get her to a place of safety within which she could engage in intensive psychotherapy. This may well have been an important factor in the lack of murderous feelings in the transference during this period of treatment. I understand that these feelings were much more present once she was in intensive therapy.

Tonnesmann (1980) approaches this same issue from the point of view of the re-enactment of traumatic infantile experience and describes how the patient can literally recreate situations which provide the opportunity to undo the traumatic past through *new experiences* within the therapeutic relationship, as well as in everyday life. Tonnesmann argues that when this happens it is the form of the therapist's actual response (based on thought and experience within the countertransference) that is decisive. The re-enactment needs to be received as a form of communication, which, she argues, is particularly common in adolescent patients with their tendency to act rather than talk about painful issues. Tonnesmann carefully distinguishes this from destructive forms of acting out.

Although she does not talk directly about the present relationship as such, Tonnesmann emphasises the experiential component of the patient-therapist interaction, and it is clear that the therapist's response must be 'enacted' rather than spoken to provide this vital therapeutic experience at this point in the treatment. Interpretation and shared understanding may well come later – if the treatment lasts long enough to permit this to happen. But, at the time that the crucial enactment takes place, 'actions' (in this specific sense) really may speak louder and more therapeutically than words. I think that this connects with the kind of well-informed therapeutic spontaneity and intuition that I referred to at the start of this chapter: 'I'm not sure if I should have done this, but . . .'. It is a form of therapeutic attunement in which, in the first instance, like is answered with like – in the same way that a playful 'conversation' between a cooing baby and an adult tends to take place in 'baby talk'.

In reflecting on the session in which Hilary was able to communicate faintly that psychiatric referral might be an option, I was not aware of any interpretations or connections that might have crystallised this tiny but crucial internal change. However, it was a very intense session from which I emerged feeling moved, tearful and relieved. I think that this reflected the intensity of the present relationship between us during the session, in which my awareness of the life-threatening danger she was in led to me being hyper-attuned to her slightest signal of a wish to change – and to live. In this respect, during the session, Hilary may have been held in a kind of emotional intensive care relationship with me. I think it is very likely that this experience bore my personal signature. I would even argue that, if I had not been able and prepared to be present for her in this way, I am not so sure that she would have been able to go through the whole excruciating but life-saving process of change that she initiated following this session.

This issue of the therapist's and the patient's authenticity within the therapeutic relationship is really at the heart of this chapter and relates to the long-standing debate about how to express this authenticity within the bounds of a carefully defined professional relationship. This becomes a particularly important consideration when authenticity is viewed as being central to the process of change emerging from the therapeutic relationship.

I know that the experiences I am describing are not just peculiar to me and my way of working and suspect that many of my colleagues act in ways which are personal to them at times, to varying degrees, depending on the therapeutic situation. While the clinical example I have chosen is at the extreme end of the spectrum of change, I have chosen it because it so clearly illustrates how terrifying change can be at any level. I think it shows how vital the therapeutic presence of an intensely attuned 'other' can be in enabling patients and indeed anyone in more everyday life, to take the first steps that lead to change, and then sustain them.

When the paper that this chapter is based on was first published, it was accompanied by commentaries from four child and adolescent psycho-therapists representing each of the main theoretical orientations of the profession – Anna Freudian (Green), Kleinian (Crockatt), Jungian (Davies) and Independent (Wilson) (Crockatt et al. 2001). It was very stimulating to read their views and to identify the strengths and weaknesses of the arguments put forward in the paper. Some of the commentators found the ideas controversial, others did not. While supporting and developing many of the ideas in the paper, Crockatt and Green both questioned whether the concept of the present relationship was necessary and pointed out that contemporary ideas about counter-transference and transference allow for transference interpretations to bear the therapist's 'personal signature'. However, while I agree that this is often true, I don't feel that this suffi-ciently helps me to understand the power of the experience that took place in the session when Hilary decided to let me contact her GP, nor indeed other powerful but wordless experiences in therapy when change has clearly taken place. I think that postulating a present relationship gives a better understanding of this clinical experience.

Davies, from a Jungian perspective, discusses the therapist's use of self in treatment and the history of this debate within analytic psychology. She quotes Fordham, who states that 'If the analyst's self is recognised it leads to a sense of security that optimally leads to greater intellectual and emotional flexibility within their personal limits' (Crockatt et al. 2001). The discussion of the dangers as well as the advantages of the therapist's use of self has long been a part of the discourse of analytic psychology. Wilson, while underlining the risks of the therapist acting out, pragmatically emphasises the importance, particularly for the adolescent, of the therapist's behaviour and the fact that thoughts about how crucial this is in treatment have been very much in the minds of many writers. These different points of view are informative as they point out not only the different perspectives that are possible, but also the similarities. What did not seem to be in question from any of the commentators was the need at times to be prag-matically prepared to take clinical 'risks', when in extremis with very distressed patients. My emphasis is on trying to understand what happens at these times and what it is that can be so instrumental in them in bringing about crucial change in the therapeutic process. For me, understanding of the transference relationship does not go far enough to explain this. When theory does not adequately fit with clinical observation, important questions are raised. The debate goes on in this book. At the time there was further discussion in the form of a response to the commentaries (Lanyado 2001c).

The actual moment when decisive change takes place is critical in determining the future path of the individual's life. A tiny change of direction can lead to an entirely different destination. For patients like Hilary, at a true crossroads in her life, massive change ensued. Psychoanalysis has always emphasised the roots of the present in the past, but the moment of change presents a paradox in which, temporarily, only the present and future matter. For our patients, at the moment of change, there is a leap into the unknown that is ultimately often risked only because of trust in the therapist as another human being. For this to happen, the patient may need to have the deeply personal experience of 'knowing' the therapist, however briefly, through the therapist's personal signature. At these perilous times, the therapist must be very present for the patient and there can be no looking back.

Chapter 8

Holding and letting go: some thoughts about ending therapy[1]

Nina Coltart (1996) has commented on the oddness of ending a (thera-peutic) relationship that is clearly so important to the patient and the way in which 'We have clothed this oddness in theory, technique and familiarity' (p. 149). She goes on to describe in detail how important the authenticity of the patient-therapist relationship is to the patient and how absorbing and central it can become in the patient's life. And then she adds: 'So what do we do? We bring it to an absolute end' (p. 150). No wonder 'good enough' as well as difficult endings are so hard to think about.

The counterpart of the patient's attachment may well be that the therapist has felt him or herself to be in the 'caregiving' role, which it is not easy to relinquish when it is time for therapy to end (Bowlby 1988; Holmes 2001). This is the aspect of the therapist's role which relates to the ordinary parental task of letting go of their child in the interests of furthering growth and development – in all the small and larger steps that are required in life.

The counterbalancing processes of holding and letting go need to be addressed so that a point is reached where ending therapy acquires the quality of 'a page in life' being turned. This is where the idea of 'transitions' rather than stark beginnings and endings can be helpful. In ordinary life, progressions cannot take place without letting go of something – whether this be the infant letting go of the breast, or letting go of the side of the pool and realising that they really can float or swim. The reality is that devel-opmental processes do not take place in isolation. Beginnings and endings belong together and remain essentially paradoxical in nature. And yet if the idea of, and capacity to, tolerate paradox during a transition can be main-tained there is a richness of experience which compensates for the anxieties that change inevitably brings to the inner world.

One of the most paradoxical and at times challenging aspects of ordinary parenting is to be able to appropriately 'let go' of a loved child, because it is

---

1 This chapter is based on the 1999 paper, 'Holding and letting go: some thoughts about the process of ending therapy', *Journal of Child Psychotherapy*, 25(3): 357–378.

developmentally timely to do so. The ebb and flow of the interrelated processes of holding and letting go is present in the parent-child relationship from the earliest days of life, and is intrinsic to the capacity to recognise separateness in the child.

This takes place within parents' understanding and capacity to respond to their child's particular strengths, weaknesses, needs and developmental stage. Once again, the idea of there being a 'season and a time for every matter under heaven' comes to mind. The balance between holding and letting go is an issue in nurturing relationships throughout life and is a reciprocal process. For example, just as the parents have to learn how and when to let go of the child and when to hold the child in mind more, so the child also needs to learn when it is safe to let go of the parents as well as when to seek the parent's presence, internally and externally. There are many life experiences which accentuate the importance of these processes – for example, weaning in infancy and leaving home during adolescence or later, illustrate the careful adjustments and readjustments in parents and child that are necessary.

For many parents there can be a profound internal contemplation and struggle with this apparently paradoxical parental task – of loving and holding a child in mind and heart, but also making every effort to let go appropriately when the latest developmental stage makes its appearance. In everyday life, many a parent facing their child's first day at school or trying to work out sensible ground rules for their rebellious adolescent can be heard to sigh and say, 'Well, you have to let them go, don't you?'. The need to accept change is particularly evident and pressing when an experience or relationship comes to an end, abruptly or with some anticipation. The process of change is inevitably deeply connected to the process of mourning and letting go of the past.

Another way of thinking developmentally about this process is in terms of the concepts, from developmental psychology, of attunement and misattunement, to which Stern (1985) has drawn attention. He describes this process as being particularly evident during the development of the sense of self and other during the first year of life – in other words, when the separateness of minds is first recognised. He argues that in order for separateness to be recognised, just the right amount of misattunement is required for the 'otherness' of the parent to be discernible. Stern shows how parents are able to 'tune' the baby 'up' or 'down' in many sensory and communicative modalities. The encouragement of separateness, with the parents' subtle, where appropriate, 'leading' of the way through deliberate misattunement, becomes the counterpart of the infant's developmental thrust towards greater independence and desire to explore. In this way parents convey that independence and separateness are safe and encouraged, while continuing to provide the secure base of attachment theory to which the child can return. This prototype of communication, which is often likened to a carefully choreographed dance, is very evident in all the small adjustments and readjustments that parents and child have to make as the child grows up. The intertwined processes of holding and letting go can also be conceptualised in this way.

Winnicott's thoughts about the gradual but necessary disillusionment of the baby, after the initial phase of life when parents make every effort to fit as closely as possible to the baby's needs, creating experiences at the start of life that he terms 'hallucinatory gratification', similarly emphasise the importance of this small but discernible gap between parents and child (Winnicott 1963). Hopkins (1996) has further emphasised the value of this lack of fit between parents and child, illustrating the ways in which 'too-good' mothering which is too well adapted to infant needs can inadvertently deprive the child of a sense of agency by 'creating a persisting state of passive merger with the mother'. Hopkins also draws attention to Winnicott's view that a similar situation can develop in therapy between therapist and patient, particularly in a therapy which becomes very difficult to end.

The parent-child relationship continues throughout life (and beyond, internally) and these same issues of separateness return again and again. They reappear when the child finds a sexual partner, when grandchildren are born, and are taken to the ultimate conclusion when facing and living through the death of the loved one – parent or child. Parents and children and, later, loved friends and partners have many opportunities in life in which to work out this complicated cocktail of separateness but inter-relatedness and, if they are able to learn from life's experiences, they get better at these difficult tasks as time goes on.

External factors determining the ending of therapy

The place of therapy in a child's and his or her family's life needs to be seen against the backcloth of the full life cycle with its many shapes and forms of relationships, as this puts the work that we do very firmly in its place. While the therapist is rightly very important to the child in the midst of therapy, part of the therapeutic task is also to find as good a way as possible to end therapy so that this ending is experienced as significant to the child and family. It is not that families are expected to live 'happily ever after', more that a process has taken place in family life through which relationships have hopefully changed for the better and the child is more securely on a healthier developmental path. The therapist has to let go of the child, and the child as well as his or her family have to let go of the therapist. In doing this the family is provided with the opportunity to think more carefully than they might have done before about what it means to move on from one phase in family life to another. They need to think about and try to be open to the process of change.

When therapy comes to an end, the complicated mix of anger, sadness, pain and regret, the inevitable feelings of there being so much left that is incomplete, are all balanced by the awareness of what has been gained through therapy, together with appropriate positive anticipation about what comes next. These feelings are intrinsic to so many life transitions. As already suggested, it can be helpful to think about the whole process of therapy and the therapeutic relationship itself as protracted transitional experiences in the Winnicottian sense (Winnicott 1951; Lanyado and Horne 1999), in which, like the loved and often essential teddy or blanket of early childhood, the therapist is vital during the central period of therapy, in times of transition, pain and anxiety but is also in time outgrown and left 'in limbo' when no longer needed. With this in mind, it can be argued that by being too focused on the finality of endings, the simultaneous beginnings of new possibilities are not sufficiently appreciated. The whole process may more usefully be thought of as another life transition, where beginnings and endings are intertwined and the paradox of transitional experience needs to be tolerated and capitalised on.

Considering the centrality of these developmental processes which relate to the ways in which important developmental stages are moved into and through, with a few notable exceptions (Salzberger-Wittenberg *et al.* 1983; Lubbe 1996; Reeves 1996; Ryz and Wilson 1999; Wittenberg 1999) there has been surprisingly little attention focused on the process of ending therapy in the literature on work with children. Does this imply an uneasiness around discussion and debate about the many ways in which children and young people's therapy comes to an end in everyday practice? Feelings of inade-quacy, guilt or even shame can arise within the therapist – perhaps along with a feeling that not enough has been done to help the child, or that colleagues would have helped the child more. This may well contribute to the lack of literature about the endings of children's and adolescents' therapy.

If there is a reluctance to think about endings, how helpful can we be to our patients for whom as good as possible an ending can be a tremendously important experience? While there is clearly a great deal to be learnt from the literature on adult patients about the processes involved in ending therapy, many of these well-recognised processes, such as separation and loss, mourning, internalisation and identification, are very readily obscured in the much more complex situation of a child ending therapy, where the presence of the environment is more forcibly felt.

The most obvious difference between a child's and an adult's treatment coming to an end is that many more external factors are likely to contribute to this decision for a child than for an adult. Most notably, the views of parents and the many different family pressures they have to balance can play an important part in deciding when therapy should stop. This may not always be the best timing when viewed purely from the child patient's point of view although, taking the whole family constellation into account, ending therapy may still be a wise decision. Indeed, from the child's point of view the decision to end may feel particularly nonsensical when he or she may have protested a great deal about coming to therapy in the first place but has nevertheless over time become very involved in the process. As one little girl so aptly and indignantly put it: 'Why do I have to stop *now*, just when I've started to enjoy it?'

There can be a counterpart in the therapist of the experience of coming to the end of a therapy which has made reasonable progress, in which the therapist also feels a very real sense of loss. To the therapist it may feel rather like leaving the theatre when a really good play has just started, probably never to know how the story continued. However, issues relating to separateness and personal identity are interwoven into the fabric of psychoanalytic psychotherapy and there is possibly no more real way in which these are faced than when the therapist and the child have to confront an ending. The child and therapist have met together for a purpose and go as far as they can together in this endeavour. Then the time comes to part and it becomes necessary to think about what resides within the child as a result of this shared experience of therapy – and also for the therapist to think about how the treatment has progressed and what they have learned from the whole experience. The therapy has to move from a situation of attentive holding at the height of its intensity, to appropriate letting go.

In a similar manner to the way in which parents have to grapple with how to facilitate separateness and independence in their children in accordance with each developmental stage, the therapist has to contemplate and think very carefully about how best to bring the experience of therapy to an end. The thoughtfulness and the painful feelings that can be aroused in the therapist during this process are not only necessary as the therapist's part of the separation experience with the particular child patient, but also represent a further working through in the therapist's internal world of his or her own experiences of separation and loss. Both of these aspects of the therapist's response in the present relationship exist alongside the continuing work in the transference.

There can often be an awareness in the child, family and therapist that later developmental stages – adolescence, becoming a parent – are likely to be difficult to negotiate and that there may well be a need for further treatment. There is always the possibility that treatment might not be available for a variety of reasons at this later stage, and this adds to the dilemma about how much therapy is 'good enough' at what might be the only time that it will be available in a person's life. However, once again it is important to be mindful of the fact that there are many ways in which people can help each other in life – psychoanalytic psychotherapy does not hold a monopoly. If a child has become more open to the positive influences that he or she encounters in life as a result of having a period of time in therapy, he or she will be able to make use of these influences in a way which was not possible prior to therapy. Just as important is an increased capacity not to get drawn into negative and destructive relationships which might repeat destructive relationships of the past. If these abilities have developed somewhat in the course of therapy, this is a very significant achievement.

In contemporary public sector treatment centres there can be severe restrictions on how many children can be offered weekly let alone more intensive treatment, and this may need to be renegotiated on a regular basis with the authorities who fund the treatment. Long waiting lists have prompted more families to seek private treatment for their children, often taking on considerable financial hardship which cannot be extended beyond what is absolutely necessary for the child's well-being. Both of these types of financial pressure add to the need to be as (therapeutically) economical as possible about treatment resources, and this inevitably means having to make the fine judgement about when a child is ready to stop therapy, despite the fact that there is still quite an element of doubt about whether the time is absolutely right. (For a fuller discussion of these issues in the context of brief work and therapeutic consultations, see Lanyado 1996, 1999b.) For 'looked after' children who have suffered such difficult starts in life, it is very hard to reach a point in therapy where there is not still a feeling in the therapist and the foster or adoptive parents that there remains much more work that needs to be done. This is why it is helpful to think in terms of seeing therapy as providing the tools for creative living for the child, together with the beginnings of some healing of traumatic experience, rather than as an endpoint where all can be resolved and repaired – which is an impossible task even in much better circumstances.

In my clinical experience, as well as from impressions gathered from colleagues and supervisees, it is unusual to have the good fortune of choosing what is felt to be, by all concerned, the right time to stop treatment. This is very different to the process of termination in adult psychoanalysis, which is what I suspect remains the unspoken prototype of how endings in child treatments 'should' be achieved. This may further contribute to the feelings of inadequacy in the child and adolescent psychotherapist when therapy seems to end 'too soon'. Endings with child patients may forcibly remind the therapist of the vulnerability and helplessness of the child patient in determining his or her own life. The child patient may need powerfully and desperately to project these feelings into the therapist when therapy has to end at a time which feels inappropriate to the pace of the therapeutic process. This may well further contribute to the feelings of helplessness and impotence engendered in the therapist in the face of some of the decisions that are made about child patients in which the therapist can have very little influence. This can be overcome to some extent, for patient and therapist, when an unplanned ending is changed in some measure into a more planned one.

In the best of circumstances, reaching an acceptable agreement between all responsible adults and the child patient about when a child is ready to think about ending therapy is likely to be a delicate process of negotiation. Has therapy achieved what it set out to achieve? How clearly was this defined in the first place, and how much have the aims of therapy been clarified or redefined as treatment has progressed? Is symptomatic change sufficient improvement if the parents or carers are finding the child much happier and easier to live with, or is evidence of deeper change essential if these improvements are to be maintained? Where significant trauma and deprivation have prompted referral, how much internal healing has taken place and is it enough to enable the child to make good use of other opportunities for growth and recovery, outside therapy? It is also very important to keep in mind the fact that parents may have changed significantly during the course of treatment and be well able to consolidate and encourage the improvements in their child in ways that they could not at the time of referral.

Even in situations where parents or carers want therapy to end because they feel it is not helping the child, and where the therapist may in some ways agree that it is best to stop treatment, bringing therapy to a planned end can be therapeutic if it provides the opportunity to face the inevitable disappointments and anger that this particular ending stirs. All these feelings, positive and negative, are grist to the mill of the process of ending.

Since beginnings and endings are so intrinsically linked in all life experience, the care taken during initial consultations in setting treatment up is ideally counterbalanced by a similarly painstaking process at the point of considering entering the last phase of therapy. While it is always advisable to talk about how therapy comes to an end when the initial treatment plan is set up, this is often forgotten by the time the possibility of ending therapy approaches. A great deal of the therapist's efforts may then be concentrated on transforming an unwisely hurried ending into a more planned and measured one in which as full an experience of 'ending' as is practically possible can be achieved. This is true, whatever the reason for ending.

The question of therapeutic aims in non-directive therapy

The whole question of the aims of non-directive therapy is rather paradoxical. We engage in a therapeutic process with the child which we know from experience can lead to greater emotional health and which will at times focus on particular areas of vulnerability as they arise in the child's material. But we cannot accurately predict what the outcome will be. Often, while making some headway in the problem that prompted the child's referral (which is notably usually made by the key adults in the child's life, not by the patient him or herself), there are lateral shoots of growth which are quite unexpected and yet are indicative of increased emotional well-being and creativity. The non-directive nature of psychoanalytic work, and if anything the 'aimlessness' of it, are what gives the work its many-layered creative and healing potential.

Of course, if one were to say this to the parents of a child (or indeed the child him or herself), they might find this statement rather odd. However, we do know from clinical experience that the non-directive process not only provides the opportunity to disentangle, interpret and dissolve symptoms, but provides many gains, particularly in the realms of increased sensitivity and capacity to think which are associated with growing emotional maturity and creativity (Lanyado and Horne 1999). These are the unforseen, more global bonuses of treatment which do not lend themselves so readily to measurement.

Even if we were able to measure accurately the level of improvement, say in the diminishment of a child's use of denial as a defence, how helpful would it really be? Where would we put the pass mark for this particular child's emotional health? At 40 per cent diminishment? At 75 per cent? At 95 per cent? The imaginary pass mark would surely need to take into account the manner in which the use of denial in this particular child's internal world balanced with the customary use of other defences, as well as the anxieties and external life pressures that the child had to live with. The complexity of obtaining valid measurements for outcome studies is well recognised (Hodges 1999).

This is not in any way to diminish the importance of undertaking outcome research where valid measurements which go beyond symptomatic change are sought. It is more to make the point that there is no clear 'finishing line' in human development and there is therefore always room for improvement. Mailer (1996) expresses this idea very powerfully when he writes 'There was that law of life so cruel and yet so just, which demanded that one must grow or else pay more for staying the same'. In this context it is worth stating the obvious: that increasing the readiness and capacity of a patient to change and be more open to life must be a central therapeutic aim. The amount of change achieved through therapy may often not be as much as has been hoped for, but it is nevertheless an important achievement and may be as far as it is possible to go at the time. As therapists, we are only too familiar with the tremendous resistances and defences that prevent change from happening, as well as the regressions which can seem to put change into reverse gear.

Post-therapy contact with child patients and their families

The question of when and how to end treatment has possibly been further compounded by some confusion over how best to follow up patients' progress over the years – both in terms of what is in the patient's best interests and in ways that would be helpful for clinical research in outcome studies. What kind of post-therapy relationship is appropriate? While good clinical practice is likely to be highly adaptive to the individual patient's needs, the view is often also expressed that an ending should be final in a way that allows appropriate feelings of mourning and loss to be fully worked through, both in the final stage of therapy and after therapy has ended.

Is it fudging the issue to carry out follow-ups and have other ways of keeping in touch with patients and their families, or can this also be of value to the patient? Without doubt, the balance between the therapist and patient gradually letting go of each other and the wish to remain in some kind of appropriate contact is difficult to achieve and varies greatly between different patient-therapist couples. Some patients keep occasional phone or letter contact with their therapist or have very occasional meetings simply to 'touch base'. Others do not have contact for years but come back for a session at a time of crisis or of achievement, which they wish to share with the therapist.

The therapist contacting the patient for research purposes – that is, as a result of the therapist's agenda, which may well be quite out of touch with the current issues in the patient's internal and external life, can have considerable clinical consequences which need to be carefully considered in each individual case. Quite apart from the intrusiveness of this kind of post-therapy approach from the therapist to the patient, the therapist may also be concerned that by remaining too present in their past patients' lives there is some acting out going on – a refusal to let go or an avoidance of the mourning process. However, there is also the opposing argument that there can be the danger of an overcompensation for this fear, resulting in the creation of an unnecessary starkness about ending therapy.

In a thought-provoking paper, Schachter et al. (1997) describe three post-termination meetings with adult analytic patients in which they argue that the traditional view that this kind of contact is undesirable is 'too narrow and unsubstantiated'. They interestingly suggest that the aim of post-termination meetings is to augment the gains of analytic work. This is certainly food for thought in terms of work with many children where by the end of treatment the therapist is a new and important person in his or her developing world. This can particularly be the case for children who are 'looked after' or who the therapist has worked with through the transition from one placement to another. For some patients and their families, post-therapy contact may play a crucial role in 'augmenting the gains' of the work – providing a secure base to return to, both in times of need and quite simply in terms of confirmation of the importance of what has taken place between them (Bowlby 1988; Edwards and Maltby 1998).

The lack of opportunity to discuss endings

A further contributing factor to the lack of discussion about ending therapy may be that there is often not sufficient opportunity during training to experience or hear about the many different ways in which therapy actually ends in ordinary clinical situations, after qualification. Quite to the contrary, during training there is often a strong anxiety about the difficulty of holding onto patients in therapy – as part of the learning process itself, as well as part of the need to meet training requirements. The idea of discussing how to work with endings can therefore feel as if it goes against the grain. During training there can be intense fears of inadequacy about whether one is really able to hold onto and help the patient. As a result, when a patient or his or her parents want to end treatment it is almost always going to feel 'too soon', so that holding onto patients rather than thinking about appropriate endings becomes much more of a preoccupation.

Endings, during training, can come to represent failure, rejection and inadequacy for the trainee. In addition, for a variety of reasons, a sizeable number of trainees may not be in supervision at the time of ending for training cases which have continued beyond training requirements, or indeed beyond qualification. This is further compounded by the fact that trainees have not had their own experience of grappling with the ending of their training analysis and have thus not had first-hand experience of what an achievement a 'good enough' ending can be. Post-qualification, with the pressures of clinical practice and responsibility, there is rarely enough time, outside privately arranged supervision, to discuss these issues in sufficient detail.

What is a 'good enough ending'?

Therapy which has progressed well can still have a conflicted ending. It is important to bear this distinction in mind as the manner in which therapy ends can overshadow a more balanced perspective of what therapy has achieved. While there may be some fantasised ideal ending that many therapists carry, which is possibly a remnant of the training school super-ego, there are some clear concerns that are reality based and to be striven for if an ending is to be as constructive as possible. In terms of therapeutic process, high on this list of the desirable qualities in a good enough ending (particularly one which is, despite all efforts to the contrary, hurried), must be a sustained attempt by the therapist to avoid the repetitious acting out of past traumatic separations and endings. If this can be achieved in some measure, despite the fact that it may leave the therapist with difficult counter-transference and personal issues to work through, it could be argued that it has been possible for the patient to learn and grow through this particular experience of ending.

The reason that I am drawing attention to this particular aspect of ending is that, if repetitions from the past are avoided to some extent, there is the possibility of a new experience of ending (and beginning) which can be thought about and verbalised in a way that is different from the past. If this provides some opportunity, even if painfully brief, to reflect on the experience of therapy and to contemplate how it feels to lose the relationship with the therapist, 'ending' will have gained a new meaning for the patient.

A difficult ending

Billy was another little boy, 4 years of age, who was referred to me for psychotherapy to help him with the transition from fostering to adoption. His therapy had helped him to part, with appropriate sadness and anger, from his long-term foster parents and gradually attach to his adoptive family. Although his therapy lasted on and off for six months after he was adopted, it became more and more difficult for his adoptive parents to bring him for his sessions, because of their ambivalence about his former life. In their need to claim Billy as their own child, they showed a tendency that is very understandable, although not always wise, to minimise the importance of all previous relationships in his life, and to confuse the harmful relationships with his natural parents with the emotional significance of his ties to his foster parents and myself. Billy's adoptive parents expressed this as a wish to put the past behind them and a clearly stated view that they were all that Billy needed to overcome his emotional difficulties – in other words, Billy needed parents, not a therapist.

While the clearest aim of Billy's therapy had been to help him through the transition into adoption, he also had serious behavioural problems arising from the early experiences of abuse and neglect that had led to his being taken into care. He was a loveable but difficult child who challenged his adoptive parents a great deal but was nearly always remorseful afterwards – just as he had been with his foster parents. While the primary aim of therapy had been achieved, it was clear that there was much more that could be done to help him. However, his adoptive parents were very clear that they wanted therapy to end and, although I managed to negotiate a few sessions, which were spaced out in time, in which to draw my relationship with Billy to a close, I witnessed some of the positive aspects of his past being downgraded and in some important respects his personal narrative of his life story being rewritten by his adoptive parents.

As I felt that part of my role with Billy had been to witness and hold the many paradoxical feelings he experienced as he moved from his foster parents to his adoptive parents, it was disturbing to see how his memories, which by then only I could authenticate, were being reshaped. This made me wonder about how secure the therapeutic gains we had made would be in the long term. However, it was vital that I kept reminding myself of whose child Billy was. He was not my child, he was his adoptive parents' child. I had to let him go. Horne (1999) has pointed out that in situations such as these, a pathological kind of holding can emerge in which the therapist can unwisely prolong an ending, in a similar way to parents who cannot let go of their child.

Despite my misgivings, it was heartening to see that, even if Billy could not openly acknowledge his positive feelings and relationships from the past, it was these internalised experiences that he was building on as his relationship with his adoptive parents grew. It is also possible that, although he could not easily talk to his adoptive parents about his memories of the loving experiences he had had with his foster family, because of the feelings of rivalry and jealousy that this stirred, he could keep these memories alive within a private area of his internal world which, in the brief opportunities he had, he shared with me.

In the incredibly difficult process of adoption, so many painful issues are alive that many defences may necessarily come into play in the child and the parents, in order to sustain the primary task of creating a new and secure attachment. The wish to cut off from the past is a very common way of dealing with the sometimes awful experiences that a loved child has had before adoption took place. This is a defence that can mellow over time, or can remain intact because the past is too painful for the child and parents to think about and threatens to disrupt the present too severely. Hunter (1999) has pointed out how important it is to work within the practical and emotional constraints of foster parents. This is also true with adoptive parents, who deserve every bit of support and respect for the immense emotional task they are undertaking.

When it was clear that Billy's therapy would come to an end, I had to struggle with my feelings of helplessness, rejection and loss, and the feeling of not having been a good enough therapist to prevent this kind of ending taking place. On reflection, this experience seemed to contain three elements. First, it reflected the adoptive parents' (and previously the foster parents') fear of having failed in their task. We all felt that we were not good enough parents and that was why Billy rejected us and was aggressive towards us at times. The feelings of failure that we all carried were in turn the result of the transference from the past of Billy's experience of having been truly failed by his birth mother in her care of him. This element of the therapeutic experience was rooted in the transference. Echoes of this failed relationship from the past remained active in the present.

Second, Billy projected into me feelings that he couldn't bear to feel for himself – his feelings of helplessness, rejection by me and his anger about this as well as his sadness about the loss. He was able to be in touch with some of these feelings, but not able to tolerate the full intensity of them. His adoptive parents' denial of the importance of therapy to him made him feel that he had to hide these feelings from them. This seemed to lead to an 'overflow' of feelings into me on the few remaining occasions that we met, and was what I needed to hold for him. These feelings, which related to the present relationship between us and the impending ending and loss of that relationship, were compounded by the complexity of his past losses and real rejections which belonged to the transference strand of the therapeutic relationship. All of these feelings remained powerfully with me long after Billy's therapy ended, and reflected my continued function of holding feelings for Billy which it remained difficult for him to hold by himself. For example, he was particularly anxious that if he expressed his anger and loss about current and past issues to his adoptive parents, they would not be able to cope with the intensity of his feelings and would reject him. This was a transference-related feeling from the past. In reality, his adoptive parents were deeply committed to him and determined to see him through whatever difficulties arose.

At the end of therapy it was as if Billy deposited as intense an experience of all these feelings with me as he could, while he still had the chance. This hopefully served the function of helping him to contain his feelings through identification with me as time went on. This identification was a consequence of the present relationship that had developed between us during his therapy.

The third way in which I had to struggle with my feelings was on a purely personal level as I reflected on what the end of Billy's therapy meant to me. It is well acknowledged that we learn something of value from each of our patients. This being so, each ending of therapy is likely to entail some working through in the therapist's internal world of the actual loss of the relationship with the patient as well as further working through of losses from the therapist's personal past. My more personal feelings also related to my real helplessness and anger that therapy was stopped 'too soon'. On reflection, I had to accept that I had to let go of Billy and had no right to insist that I knew better than his adoptive parents about what was best for their child. While I did this with as much grace as I could at the end of his therapy, it took me a while truly to achieve this within myself.

I learnt a lot from this ending, technically, in terms of case management, and in terms of the importance of constructive 'letting go' as the most helpful thing that the therapist can do in these difficult situations. Part of my difficulty in letting go of Billy was a facet of the present relationship we had formed. It was a sign that his therapy mattered to me as well as to him. Within the present relationship strand of the therapeutic relationship my difficulty in letting go could be understood as me experiencing what his birth parents had been unable to feel. There are many therapists who openly admit to feeling sad and tearful at the end of a child or young person's therapy.

Of course Billy was unaware that I felt we were finishing therapy too quickly, but talking about the sad feelings that we both felt because it was time for him to end his therapy was important to him as it confirmed to him that he could evoke caring feelings in others. Where therapy has been a significant experience for therapist and patient, this real sense of loss in the therapist is not in my view 'unprofessional', but a reflection of the authenticity of what has been shared but which, therapeutically, also needs to be let go of.

My sadness and difficulty over letting go of Billy, together with my efforts to get as much time as possible in which to bring therapy to an end, also avoided repetition of the traumatic ending he had had with his birth mother. The fact that his ending with his foster mother had been so well worked with had already broken the potential for repetition. I needed to do my best to ensure that my ending with Billy provided further experience of sad farewells rather than rejection. The sadness that was experienced could be talked about and put to therapeutic use.

Looking back on how the therapy of the children referred to in this book ended, it is striking that apart from Billy, they all ended for external reasons – such as transfer to secondary education, or leaving the residential unit in which they were having therapy. The external reasons provided a sensible time scale – usually of about six months – with which to work with the feelings around ending, and felt appropriate in the fuller pattern of the child's life at the time.

This sense of having only a limited time span in which to work is common in work with children and adolescents and is why so often the therapeutic work may not have been able to reach some very important issues in the patient's life. The patient was simply not ready at the time to explore these areas. This is why taking a view of therapy as a process which facilitates a creative mind that is increasingly able to cope with change, as opposed to being fearful of it, is so valuable. Therapy can provide some of the essential tools with which to work at the many problems that life throws up. Above all, it is these ways of living that the patient takes with him or her when therapy ends.

In so many ways, as psychoanalytical psychotherapists, we can only accompany our patients on a small section of their journey through life and, while we are with them, do the best we can to bring about some personal growth. We prepare the ground and provide some of the nutrients which help the patient to find a way of tuning in to the life-enhancing processes which are all around us. Helping patients to have a good enough ending whatever the difficulty of the circumstances is no different from the many difficult tasks that parents have in order to see their children through in everyday life. Being aware of the role that 'letting go' plays in this process can only enhance the quality of the experience.

References

Ainsworth, M. (1982) 'Attachment: retrospect and prospect', in C. M. Parkes and J. Stevenson-Hinde (eds) *The Place of Attachment in Human Behaviour*. London: Tavistock.

Alvarez, A. (1989) 'Development towards the latency period: splitting and the need to forget in borderline children', *Journal of Child Psychotherapy*, 15(2): 71–83.

Alvarez, A. (1992) *Live Company: Psychoanalytic Psychotherapy with Autistic, Borderline, Deprived and Abused Children*. London: Tavistock/Routledge.

Alvarez, A. (2000) 'Moral imperatives with borderline children: the grammar of wishes and the grammar of needs', in J. Symington (ed.) *Imprisoned Pain and its Transformation: A Festschrift for H. Sidney Klein*. London: Karnac.

Alvarez, A. and Reid, S. (eds) (1999) *Autism and Personality: Findings from the Tavistock Autism Workshop*. London: Routledge.

Baker, R. (1993) 'The patient's discovery of the psychoanalyst as a new object', *International Journal of Psycho-Analysis*, 74: 1223–9.

Balint, M. (1968) *The Basic Fault*. London: Tavistock.

Baradon, T. *et al.* (2001) Video presentation at ACP conference.

Bergman, M. S. and Jucovy M. E. (1982) *Generations of the Holocaust*. New York: Basic Books.

Bick, E. (1968) 'The experience of the skin in early object relations', *International Journal of Psycho-Analysis*, 49.

Bion, W. R. (1962a) 'The psychoanalytic study of thinking, 11', *International Journal of Psycho-Analysis*, 43.

Bion, W. R. (1962b) *Learning from Experience*. London: Heinemann.

Bion, W. R. (1967) 'Notes on memory and desire', *The Psychoanalytic Forum*, 272–3, 279–80.

Boston, M. and Szur, R. (eds) (1983) *Psychotherapy with Severely Deprived Children*. London: Routledge & Kegan Paul.

Bowlby, J. (1988) *A Secure Base: Clinical Applications of Attachment Theory*. London: Routledge.

Brazelton, T. (1984) *The Neo-natal Behavioural Assessment Scale* (Clinics in Developmental Medicine, No.88). London: International Medical Publications.

Byng-Hall, J. (1995) 'Security in the family', in J. Byng-Hall, *Improvising Family Scripts: Improvisation and Systems Change*. New York: Guilford Press.

Cant, D. (2002) 'Joined-up psychotherapy: the place of individual psychotherapy in residential therapeutic provision for children', *Journal of Child Psychotherapy*, 28(3): 267–81.

Carlberg, G. (1997) 'Laughter opens the door: turning points in child psychotherapy', *Journal of Child Psychotherapy*, 23: 3.

Carpy, D. V. (1989) 'Tolerating the counter-transference: a mutative process', *International Journal of Psycho-Analysis*, 70(2): 287–94.

Casement, P. (2002) *Learning from Our Mistakes: Beyond Dogma in Psychoanalysis and Psychotherapy*. Hove, East Sussex: Brunner-Routledge.

Chasseguet-Smirgel, J. (1983) 'Perversion and the universal law', in J. Chasseguet-Smirgel, *Creativity and Perversion*. London: Free Association Books.

Coltart, N. (1996) *The Baby and the Bathwater*. London: Karnac.

Crockatt, G., Davies, M., Green, V. and Wilson, P. (2001) 'Commentaries on "The symbolism of the story of Lot and his wife"', *Journal of Child Psychotherapy*, 27(1): 35–46.

Daws, D. (1989) *Through the Night: Helping Parents and Sleepless Infants*. London: Free Association Books.

Daws, D. (1999) 'Brief psychotherapy with infants and their parents', in M. Lanyado and A. Horne (eds) *The Handbook of Child and Adolescent Psychotherapy: Psychoanalytic Approaches*. London: Routledge.

Dockar-Drysdale, B. (1990) *The Provision of the Primary Experience: Winnicottian Work with Children and Adolescents*. London: Free Association Books.

Edwards, J. and Maltby, J. (1998) 'Holding the child in mind: work with parents and families in a consultation service', *Journal of Child Psychotherapy*, 24(1): 109–33.

Emanuel, R. (1996) 'Psychotherapy with children traumatised in infancy', *Journal of Child Psychotherapy*, 22(2): 214–39.

Emanuel, R. (2001) 'A-void – an exploration of defenses against sensing nothingness', *International Journal of Psycho-Analysis*, 82: 1069.

Fleming, R. (2002) Personal communication.

Fransman, T. (2002) 'On gaps and spaces', paper presented to the Scottish Association of Psychoanalytic Psychotherapists.

Freud, S. (1910) *The Future Prospects of Psycho-analytic Theory*, standard edn, Vol. 11.

Gabbard, G. (2000) 'Disguise or consent: problems and recommendations concerning the publication of clinical material', *International Journal of Psycho-Analysis*, 81(6).

Garland, C. (ed.) (1998) *Understanding Trauma. A Psychoanalytic Approach*. London: Duckworth.

Greenson, R. and Wexler, M. (1969) 'The non-transference relationship in the psychoanalytic situation', *International Journal of Psycho-Analysis*, 50: 27–39.

Grossman, D. (1994) *The Book of Intimate Grammar*. London: Picador.

Grunbaum, L. (1997) 'Psychotherapy with children in refugee families who have survived torture: containment and understanding of repetitive behaviour and play', *Journal of Child Psychotherapy*, 23(3): 437–52.

Hamilton, V. (1996) *The Analyst's Pre-Conscious*. Hillsdale, NJ: The Analytic Press.

Hartnup, T. (1986) 'Children and institutions II: the professional and the institution', *Journal of Child Psychotherapy*, 12(2): 41–54.

Heimann, P. (1950) 'On counter-transference', *International Journal of Psycho-Analysis*, 31: 81–4.

Hindle, D. (2001) 'An intensive assessment of a small sample of siblings placed in foster care', PhD thesis, University of East London and Tavistock Clinic Library.

Hodges, J. (1999) 'Research in child and adolescent psychotherapy: an overview', in M. Lanyado and A. Horne (eds) *The Handbook of Child and Adolescent Psychotherapy: Psychoanalytic Approaches*. London: Routledge.

Hodges, J., Lanyado, M. and Andreou, C. (1994) 'Sexuality and violence: preliminary clinical hypotheses from the psychotherapeutic assessments in a research programme on young sexual offenders', *Journal of Child Psychotherapy*, 20(3): 283–308.

Holmes, J. (1998) 'The changing aims of psychoanalytic psychotherapy: an integrative approach', *International Journal of Psycho-Analysis*, 79: 227–40.

Holmes, J. (2001) *The Search for the Secure base: Attachment Theory and Psychotherapy*. London: Brunner-Routledge.

Hopkins, J. (1984) 'The probable role of trauma in a case of foot and shoe fetishism: aspects of psychotherapy of a six year old girl', *Journal of Child Psychotherapy*, 11: 79–91.

Hopkins, J. (1986) 'Solving the mystery of monsters: steps towards the recovery from trauma', *Journal of Child Psychotherapy*, 12(1): 61–71.

Hopkins, J. (1992) 'Infant-parent psychotherapy', *Journal of Child Psychotherapy*, 18: 5–17.

Hopkins, J. (1996) 'The dangers and deprivations of too-good mothering', *Journal of Child Psychotherapy*, 22(3): 407–22.

Hopkins, J. (2000) 'Overcoming a child's resistance to late adoption: how one attachment can facilitate another', *Journal of Child Psychotherapy*, 26(3): 335–47.

Horne, A. (1999) 'Normal emotional development', in M. Lanyado and A. Horne (eds) *The Handbook of Child and Adolescent Psychotherapy: Psychoanalytic Approaches*. London: Routledge.

Horne, A. (2001) 'Brief communications from the edge: psychotherapy with challenging adolescents', *Journal of Child Psychotherapy*, 27(1): 3–18.

Hunter, M. (1999) 'The child and adolescent psychotherapist in the community', in M. Lanyado and A. Horne (eds) *The Handbook of Child and Adolescent Psychotherapy: Psychoanalytic Approaches*. London: Routledge.

Hunter, M. (2001) *Psychotherapy with Young People in Care: Lost and Found*. London: Brunner-Routledge.

Hurry, A. (ed.) (1998) *Psychoanalysis and Developmental Therapy*. London: Karnac.

Infant Mental Health Journal (1998) Special edition: 'Interventions that effect change in psychotherapy: a model based on infant research', 19(3).

Ironside, L. (2002) 'Living in a storm: an examination of the impact of deprivation and abuse on the psychotherapeutic process and the implications for clinical practice', PhD thesis, University of East London and Tavistock Clinic Library.

Journal of Child Psychotherapy (2000) Special edition: 'Fostering and adoption', 26(3).

Jung, C. G. (ed.) (1964) *Man and his Symbols*. London: Aldus Books.

Kernberg, O. (1975) *Borderline Conditions and Pathological Narcissism*. New York: Aronsson Inc.

Khan, M. M. R. (1979a) 'Intimacy, complicity and mutuality in perversions', in

M. M. R. Khan, *Alienation in Perversions*. London: The Hogarth Press and The Institute of Psycho-Analysis.

Khan, M. M. R. (1979b) 'From masochism to psychic pain', in M. M. R. Khan, *Alienation in Perversions*. London: The Hogarth Press and The Institute of Psycho-Analysis.

Klein, J. (2003) *Jacob's Ladder: Essays on Experiences of the Ineffable in the Context of Contemporary Psychotherapy*. London: Karnac.

Klein, M. (1932) 'Neurosis in children', in M. Klein, *The Psycho-Analysis of Children*. London: The Hogarth Press and The Institute of Psycho-Analysis.

Klein, M. (1946) 'Notes on some schizoid mechanisms', in *Collected Works*, vol. III. London: The Hogarth Press and The Institute of Psycho-Analysis.

Lanyado, M. (1985) 'Surviving Trauma – dilemmas in the psychotherapy of traumatised children', *British Journal of Psychotherapy*, 2(1), and *Bulletin of the British Association of Psychotherapists*, July: 50–62.

Lanyado, M. (1987) 'Asymbolic and symbolic play: developmental perspectives in the treatment of disturbed children', *Journal of Child Psychotherapy*, 13(2): 33–44.

Lanyado, M. (1988) 'Working with anxiety in a residential special primary school', *Maladjustment and Therapeutic Education*, 6(1): 36–48.

Lanyado, M. (1989a) 'United we stand . . .? Stress in residential work with disturbed children', *Maladjustment and Therapeutic Education*, 7(3): 136–46.

Lanyado, M. (1989b) 'Variations on a theme of transference and counter-transference', *Journal of Child Psychotherapy*, 15(2): 85–102.

Lanyado, M. (1991a) 'Putting theory into practice: working with perversion and chaos in the analytic process', *Journal of Child Psychotherapy*, 17(1): 25–40.

Lanyado, M. (1991b) 'On creating a psychotherapeutic space', *Journal of Social Work Practice*, 5(1): 31–40.

Lanyado, M. (1993) 'Stress – an occupational hazard of working with disturbed children', *Educational Therapy and Therapeutic Teaching*, 1(2): 23–38.

Lanyado, M. (1996) 'Winnicott's Children: the holding environment and therapeutic communication in brief and non-intensive work', *Journal of Child Psychotherapy*, 22(3): 423–43.

Lanyado, M. (1997) 'Memories in the making: the experience of moving from fostering to adoption for a five year-old-boy', *Journal of the British Association of Psychotherapists*, December: 3–18.

Lanyado, M. (1999a) 'Holding and letting go: some thoughts about the process of ending therapy', *Journal of Child Psychotherapy*, 25(3): 357–78.

Lanyado, M. (1999b) 'Brief psychotherapy and therapeutic consultations: how much therapy is good enough?', in M. Lanyado and A. Horne (eds) *The Handbook of Child and Adolescent Psychotherapy: Psychoanaylytic Approaches*. London: Routledge, pp. 231–46.

Lanyado, M. (1999c) 'The treatment of traumatisation in children', in M. Lanyado and A. Horne (eds) *The Handbook of Child and Adolescent Psychotherapy: Psychoanalytic Approaches*. London: Routledge, pp. 275–91.

Lanyado, M. (2000) 'Fenomeni transizionali e cambiamento psichico: Riflessioni sul ruolo del transfert e della relazione attuale nel passagio dall affidamento all adozione' ['Transitional phenomena and psychic change: the role of transference and the new relationship as seen in the therapy of children moving from fostering to adoption'], *Studi Psicoanalitici del Bambino e dell Adolescente*, 8(3): 283–93.

Lanyado, M. (2001a) 'Daring to try again: the hope and pain of forming new attachments', *Therapeutic Communities*, 22(1): 5–18.

Lanyado, M. (2001b) 'The symbolism of the story of Lot and his wife: the function of the "present relationship" and non-interpretative aspects of the therapeutic relationship in facilitating change', *Journal of Child Psychotherapy*, 27(1): 19–33.

Lanyado, M. (2001c) Letter to the Editors: 'Transition and change: a response to commentaries on "The symbolism of the story of Lot and his wife"', *Journal of Child Psychotherapy*, 27(2): 226–30.

Lanyado, M. (2002) 'Creating transitions in the lives of children suffering from "multiple traumatic loss"', in L. Caldwell (ed.) *The Elusive Child*. London: Karnac, pp. 93–112.

Lanyado, M. (2003a) 'The emotional tasks of moving from fostering to adoption: transitions, attachment, separation and loss', *Clinical Child Psychology and Psychiatry* (special edition on fostering and adoption), 8(3): 337–49.

Lanyado, M. (2003b) 'The roots of mental health: emotional development and the caring environment', in J. Pooley, A. Ward, K. Kasinski and A. Worthington (eds) *Therapeutic Communities for Children and Young People*. London: Jessica Kingsley, pp. 65–81.

Lanyado, M., Hodges, J., Bentovim, A., Andreou, C., Williams, B. (1995) 'Understanding boys who sexually abuse other children: a clinical illustration', *Psychoanalytic Psychotherapy*, 9(3): 231–42.

Lanyado, M. and Horne, A. (1999) 'The therapeutic relationship and process', in M. Lanyado and A. Horne (eds) *The Handbook of Child and Adolescent Psychotherapy: Psychoanalytic Approaches*. London: Routledge, pp. 56–72.

Lubbe, T. (1996) 'Who lets go first? Some observations on the struggles around weaning', *Journal of Child Psychotherapy*, 22(2): 195–213.

McFarland Solomon, H. and Twyman, M. (eds) (2003) *Ethics In Contemporary Analytic Practice*. London: Free Association Books.

Maher, A. (1999) 'Using a therapeutic model of thought and practice' in A. Hardwick and J. Woodhead (eds) *Loving, Hating and Survival*. Brookfield, VT: Ashgate Publishing.

Mailer, N. (1976) *The Presidential Papers*. London: Grafton.

Meltzer, D. (1967) *The Psychoanalytic Process*. Strath Tay: Clunie.

Melzack, S. (1999) 'Psychotherapeutic work with child and adolescent refugees from political violence', in M. Lanyado and A. Horne (eds) *The Handbook of Child and Adolescent Psychotherapy: Psychoanalytic Approaches*. London: Routledge.

Mendelsohn, A. (1997) 'Pervasive traumatic loss from AIDS in the life of a four year old African boy', *Journal of Child Psychotherapy*, 23(3): 399–415.

Meng, M. and Freud, E. (eds) (1963) *Psychoanalysis and Faith: The Letters of Sigmund Freud and Oscar Pfister*. New York: Basic Books.

Menzies Lyth, I. (1988) *Containing Anxiety in Institutions. Selected Essays*, vol. 1. London: Free Association Books.

Miller, A. (1987) *The Drama of Being a Child*. London: Virago.

Molino, A. (ed.) (1997) *Freely Associated: Encounters in Psychoanalysis with Christopher Bollas, Joyce McDougall, Michael Eigen, Adam Philips and Nina Coltart*. London: Free Association Books.

Molino, A. (1999) *The Couch and the Tree: Dialogues in Psychoanalysis and Buddhism*. London: Constable.

Mollon, P. (1996) *Multiple Selves, Multiple Voices: Working with Trauma, Violation and Dissociation*. Chichester: Wiley.

Money-Kyrle, R. (1977) 'On being a psycho-analyst', in *The Collected Papers of Roger Money-Kyrle*. Strath Tay: Clunie Press.

Ogden, T. H. (1979) 'On projective identification', *International Journal of Psycho-Analysis*, 60.

Ogden, T. H. (1999) *Reverie and Interpretation. Sensing Something Human*. London: Karnac.

Pally, R. (2000) *The Mind-Brain Relationship*. London: Karnac.

Perry, B. D., Pollard, R., Blakey, T., Baker, W. and Vigilant, D. (1995) 'Childhood trauma, the neurobiology of adaptation and "user-dependent" development of the brain: how "states" become "traits"', *Infant Mental Health Journal*, 16(4): 271–91.

Pynoos, R. (1992) 'Grief trauma in children and adolescents', *Bereavement Care*, 11(1): 2.

Racker, H. (1957) 'The meanings and uses of counter-transference', in *Transference and Counter-Transference*. London: Karnac.

Raphael-Leff, J. (2002) *Parent-Infant Psychodynamics: Wild Things, Mirror and Ghosts*. London: Whurr.

Reeves, C. (1996) 'Transition and transience: Winnicott on leaving and dying', *Journal of Child Psychotherapy*, 22(3): 444–55.

Ryz, P. and Wilson, G. (1999) 'Endings as gain', *Journal of Child Psychotherapy*, 25(3): 379–403.

Salzberger-Wittenberg, I., Henry G. and Osborne, E. (1983) *The Emotional Experience of Teaching and Learning*. London: Routledge.

Sandler, A.-M., (1988) 'Comments on therapeutic and countertherapeutic factors in psychoanalytic technique', *Bulletin of the Anna Freud Centre*, 11(1).

Schachter, J., Martin G. C., Gundle M. J. and O'Neil, M. K. (1997) 'Clinical experience with psychoanalytic post-termination meetings', *International Journal of Psycho-Analysis*, 78(6): 1183–98.

Schore, A. N. (1994) *Affect Regulation and the Origin of the Self*. Hillsdale, NJ: Lawrence Erlbaum.

Schore, A. N. (2002) Contribution to the forum on 'A psychoanalytic view of relational trauma' at the 50th Anna Freud Colloquium, International Parent-Infant Study Day, London, November.

Sinason, V. (1988) 'Dolls and bears: from symbolic equation to symbol – the use of different play material for sexually abused children', *British Journal of Psychotherapy*, 4(4).

Sinason, V. (1991) 'Interpretations that feel horrible to make and theoretical unicorn', *Journal of Child Psychotherapy*, 17(1): 11–24.

Sinason, V. (ed.) (1994) *Treating Survivors of Satanist Abuse*. London: Routledge.

Sinason, V. (1999) 'The psychotherapeutic needs of the learning disabled and multiply disabled child', in M. Lanyado and A. Horne (eds) *The Handbook of Child and Adolescent Psychotherapy. Psychoanalytic Approaches*. London: Routledge.

Skuse, D., Bentovim, A., Hodges, J., Stevenson, J., Andreou, C., Lanyado, M.,

New, M., Williams, B. and McMillan, D. (1997) *The Influence of Early Experience of Sexual Abuse on the Formation of Sexual preferences in Adolescence.* Research report by Behavioural Sciences Unit, Institute of Child Health, commissioned by the Department of Health.

Skuse, D., Bentovim, A., Hodges, J., Stevenson, J., Andreou, C., Lanyado, M., New, M., Williams, B. and McMillan, D. (1998) 'Risk factors for development of sexually abusive behaviour in sexually victimised adolescent boys: cross sectional study', *British Medical Journal*, 317: 175–79.

Solomon, J. and George, C. (eds) (1999) *Attachment Disorganisation.* London: Guilford Press.

Sprince, J. (2000) 'Towards an integrated network', *Journal of Child Psychotherapy*, 26(3): 413–31.

Sprince, J. (2002) 'Developing containment: psychoanalytic consultancy to a therapeutic community for traumatised children', *Journal of Child Psychotherapy*, 28(2): 147–61.

Stern, D. (1985) *The Interpersonal World of the Infant: A View from Psychoanalysis and Developmental Psychology.* New York: Basic Books.

Stern, D., Sander, L., Nahum, J., Harrison, A., Lyons-Ruth, K., Morgan, A., Bruschweiler-Stern, N. and Tronick, E. (1998) 'Non-intepretive mechanisms in psychoanalytic therapy: the "something more" than interpretation', *International Journal of Psycho-Analysis*, 79: 903–21.

Sternberg, J. (2003) 'An examination of the relevance of the study of infant observation to psychoanalytic psychotherapy trainings'. Tavistock Clinic and University of East London.

Symington, N. (1986) 'The analyst's act of freedom as agent of therapeutic change', in G. Kohon (ed.) *The British School of Psychoanalysis: The Independent Tradition.* London: Free Association Books.

Tonnesmann, M., (1980) 'Adolescent re-enactment, trauma and reconstruction', *Journal of Child Psychotherapy*, 11: 23–44.

Tronick, E. Z. (2003) 'Of course all relationships are unique: how co-creative processes generate unique mother-infant and parent-therapist relationships and change other relationships', *Psychoanalytic Inquiry*, 23(3): 473–91.

Tsiantis, J., Boethius, S., Hallerfors, B., Horne, A. and Tischler, T. (2000) *Work with Parents: Psychoanalytic Psychotherapy with Children and Adolescents.* London: Karnac.

Tuckett, D. (2000) 'Reporting clinical events in the journal: towards the construction of a special case', *International Journal of Psycho-Analysis*, 81: 1065.

Tustin, F. (1981) *Autistic States in Children.* London: Routledge & Kegan Paul.

Tustin, F. (1990) *The Protective Shell in Children and Adults.* London: Karnac.

Tustin F. (1992) *Autistic States in Children.* London: Routledge.

Ward, A., Kasinski, K., Pooley. J. and Worthington, A. (eds) (2003) *Therapeutic Communities for Children and Young People.* London: Jessica Kingsley.

Ward, A. and McMahon, L. (1998) *Intuition is not Enough: Matching Learning with Practice in Therapeutic Child Care.* London: Routledge.

Wilson, P. (1989) 'Latency and certainty', *Journal of Child Psychotherapy*, 15(2): 59–69.

Winnicott, D. W. (1947) 'Hate in the counter-transference', in D. W. Winnicott

(1958) *Collected Papers: From Paediatrics to Psycho-Analysis*. London: Tavistock.

Winnicott, D. W. (1951) 'Transitional objects and transitional phenomena', in D. W. Winnicott (1971) *Playing and Reality*. Harmondsworth: Pelican.

Winnicott, D. W. (1956) 'Primary maternal preoccupation', in D. W. Winnicott (1958) *Collected Papers: From Paediatrics to Psycho-Analysis*. London: Tavistock.

Winnicott, D. W. (1958) 'The capacity to be alone', in D. W. Winnicott (1965) *The Maturational Processes and the Facilitating Environment*. London: Hogarth.

Winnicott, D. W. (1963) 'From dependence towards independence in the development of the individual', in D. W. Winnicott (1965) *The Maturational Processes and the Facilitating Environment*. London: Hogarth.

Winnicott, D. W. (1971) *Playing and Reality*. London: Tavistock.

Wittenberg, I. (1999) 'Ending therapy', *Journal of Child Psychotherapy*, 25(3): 339–56.

Woodhead, J. (2002) Video presentation at AFC parent infant day, November 2002, London.

Index

action, therapy through 72
acting out: therapeutic 109, 113, 114; by
  therapist 52, 104, 115
adoption *see* looked after children;
  transition
affect regulation 16, 24, 80
aims, therapeutic 123–4
aloneness 20; in presence of other 24, 35,
  82, 91, 92, 105–6
Amy (case study) 76
attachment theory 20, 21, 82, 118
attachments: disrupted 30, 87, 89, 128;
  to therapist 117
attunement, therapeutic 7, 10, 16, 21,
  106, 114, 118
autistic patients 7

babies: deprivation 94; disillusionment
  119; feelings 52; and maternal stress
  47–9
Balint, M. 20, 35
basic fault, healing 20, 35
Billy (case study) 127–30; *see also*
  ending therapy
Bion, W.R. 11
bodily feelings 15
body language *see* communication,
  non-verbal
The Book of Intimate Grammar 18
boundaries: breaching 40, 46, 64, 65,
  67–71, 104; limitations 104;
  professional 44; setting 5, 57; in
  therapeutic units 58, 59; transitional
  space 82
Bowlby, J. 20, 92
brain function, and trauma 19
brief communications 108, 109, 112, 114

carrying, psychological 106–12; *see also*
  containment; holding; pocket
  metaphor
change: capacity for 124, 130; case
  studies 26–8; difficulties 77, 107,
  115; crossroads 116; fear 9, 75, 107,
  115, 116, 130; incremental 6, 8, 9,
  35, 86; measurement 124; and
  moments-of-meeting 106; and
  mourning/letting go 118; potential
  12; processes 7, 83–4, 106, 119;
  psychic 15, 86; regressive 81, 124;
  resistance 124; sudden/noisy 9, 35,
  36; therapeutic 5–8; window of
  opportunity 107, 109–10; *see also*
  healing; transition
Chasseguet-Smirgel, J. 62, 69, 70
chrysalis symbol 25, 26
codes of conduct 6
communication/s: brief 108, 109, 112,
  114; case studies 63, 67, 68;
  emotional 41; non-verbal 4, 16, 20,
  22, 23, 25, 32, 41, 42, 57, 108, 111,
  113, 115; transference 68;
  unconscious 52
communities *see* therapeutic units/
  communities
confidentiality, looked after children
  xiii–xiv, 59, 97–9, 108–9
conflict, core, case study 52, 55
containment 113; babies 48, 49; case
  studies 24, 25–6, 30, 32, 34; trauma
  24–6
continuity, promoting 75
counter-transference 23, 39; classical
  view 40; negative 51, 52; positive
  42–5, 49, 50; and present relationship
  40; and projection 40, 41; and